The
WINE-TASTING CLASS

THE
WINE-TASTING CLASS

EXPERTISE IN 12 TASTINGS

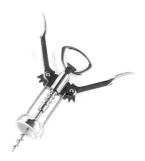

JUDY RIDGWAY

FOREWORD BY FRANCIS FORD COPPOLA

CLARKSON POTTER/PUBLISHERS
New York

Published by Clarkson N. Potter/Publishers,
201 East 50th Street, New York, New York 10022.
Member of the Crown Publishing Group.

Random House, Inc. New York, Toronto, London, Sydney, Auckland

http://www.randomhouse.com/

Conceived and produced by Breslich & Foss Limited, London.

CLARKSON N. POTTER, POTTER,
and colophon are trademarks of Clarkson N. Potter, Inc.

Printed in Hong Kong

Library of Congress Cataloging-in-Publication Data is available upon request.

ISBN 0-517-70559-1

10 9 8 7 6 5 4 3 2

First American Edition

CONTENTS

I think fine food and wine have almost magical properties that promote health; to me the coming together of friends to enjoy a fine meal of authentic food and quality wines reduces stress and augments happiness. No doubt this dates back to my childhood. The happiest times for me were those holidays such as Thanksgiving and Christmas and other occasions—birthdays, anniversaries, or just basic family get-togethers—when all my uncles, aunts, and cousins came to our home and there was laughter and plenty of kids and people were united around the table with these extraordinary Italian dishes and the wine would flow.

During Prohibition, my family made wine right in their basement in New York City, in a big concrete fermenter they built themselves. My grandfather would buy a boxcar load of grapes from the Napa Valley with his brothers and he would give a gallon of wine to absolutely everybody. It was not very good wine, I was told by my father; it was what I would call a thrifty wine.

Of course since then I've had the opportunity to sample many of the world's great wines. Yet to this day I don't consider myself a connoisseur—I'm still discovering myself, my own opinion, how it changes, and how wines I didn't enjoy that much or found astringent, or unapproachable, two years later—or sometimes even an hour later—I find extremely enjoyable and rewarding. When it comes to wines, people are very circumspect about giving their opinions, but I always try to encourage them: Just say what you like. Taste many wines, consider which seems most pleasing to your palate, and learn about the different factors that affect how a wine tastes. There is so much in a glass of wine, in its color, its aroma, and in its taste that tells of its heritage, of the land it comes from, the weather, of the philosophy of the family and the company making it. As a winemaker I've become very conscious of how the decisions you make in caring for the vineyard and in planting the vines, of course, as well as in ageing and cellaring the wine, affect what finally ends up in the glass. Eleanor and I have the privilege of being the conservators of one of America's great wine estates, founded by Gustave Niebaum in 1879. Under the Niebaum-Coppola name we continue Niebaum's tradition of excellence and dedication to the land.

When it comes to selecting and appreciating wines I definitely lead with my feelings more often than my brain. But my feelings have always given good guidance. Learn to follow yours, and you will find that you'll be rewarded with many pleasurable and enriching occasions that come from the combination of food, friends and a good wine.

FRANCIS FORD COPPOLA

INTRODUCTION

This book is based on the notion that the best way to learn about wine is by tasting and enjoying it. After all, it is much more fun actually to experience the differences than just to read about them. Tasting brings the subject to life, offering an interesting way of finding answers to many of the questions commonly asked by those who are keen to develop their appreciation of wine.

The tastings are designed to build both knowledge and ability, so that by the end of the book you are certain to know a good deal more about wine than you did at the start. You will better understand why you like or dislike certain wines, and will learn how to express those preferences.

In Tasting 1 you will practice the basic tasting procedure and begin to think critically about appearance and color, aroma, and palate. Tastings 2 to 5 look at the specific attributes of sweetness and acidity, fruit flavors, wood, body, tannin, alcohol, and overall balance. In Tasting 6 you will have the opportunity to assess your progress before moving on to Tastings 7 and 8, which examine the importance of particular vintages and regions. In Tastings 9 and 10 rosé and sparkling wines are assessed, and in Tastings 11 and 12 the mysteries of matching wine to food are unraveled.

You can, of course, go through the tastings by yourself or with a partner, but it is also great fun to work with a small group of interested friends. You might spend time reading a section, tasting the wines, then savoring them with an appropriate meal. (If you have dinner before the tasting, try not to finish the meal with anything very sweet, as this will affect your palate for some time afterwards. Spirits can also affect the subsequent taste of wine, so avoid drinking these immediately before the tasting.)

The looseleaf notebook that accompanies *The Wine-Tasting Class* will become your personal record of the wines tasted. Such a record will prove invaluable when deciding on wines to buy for the future, and when choosing wines to serve with particular foods. You can also cross-reference the wines sampled in the tastings with the notes that you write up in the notebook. Thus if you want to jog your memory as to how a particular wine tastes you need only look for the appropriate tasting reference in your notes.

BUYING THE WINE

Each tasting includes a list of the wines you will need. The list usually specifies the wine-producing areas from which the wine should come and may indicate the grape varieties. It does not designate the producer so you have quite a lot of discretion in your choice of wine. In some cases, you will be able to use a wine sampled in an earlier tasting, and this is indicated in the text.

If the list specifies an Australian Chardonnay you are free to chose an expensive estate-bottled wine or a more reasonably priced bottle. Your choice will, of course, depend upon what is available locally. If there is more than one example of the listed wine in the store, ask your wine merchant which wine is considered to be the most typical of the region.

It is worth remembering that while the most expensive wine is not necessarily the best, the cheapest will almost certainly be the worst. A certain percentage of the price goes on the bottle, cork and label, and another percentage to pay the middlemen and taxes. On a cheap bottle of wine this does not leave very much for the producer.

The most inexpensive wines are often branded wines from large commercial producers. They are blends designed to taste much the same year in, year out. In America these wines often have names such as "Chablis" or "Red Burgundy," even though they do not come from those areas and are not made from the grape varieties that would be used there. In Australia the situation used to be the same, but these names are gradually being phased out. Once exported to Europe, these blends are simply labeled "Californian Red Wine," or "Australian White Wine" because specific names are allowed only if the wines really do come from the areas on the label. They can be quite good

---

OLD WORLD / NEW WORLD

Wine enthusiasts often use the expression "old world wine" as shorthand for all European wines, and "new world wine" as shorthand for the wines of newer wine producing regions such as America, Australia and New Zealand, South Africa, Chile and Argentina. These terms are used throughout the book.

and would be a suitable choice for a tasting that suggested a light red or white wine.

Supermarkets and stores are likely to offer lower prices than wine merchants or mail-order firms, but they do not deliver and their sales staff are rarely very well informed about wine. The advantage of specialist wine merchants is that they provide a personal service. You can talk to knowledge-able people who will be able to give advice on the range of wines on offer.

Buying wine by mail order demands no effort, but for free delivery you may have to commit yourself to two or three cases of untasted wine. This is fine if you know and trust the company, but could be risky if you do not.

STORING THE WINE

If you buy wine in advance and keep it at home, store the bottles on their sides. This keeps the corks in contact with the wine and prevents them from drying out. If the corks do dry out they may shrink, thus allowing air to come into contact with the wine and

CHECKLIST FOR A WINE TASTING

- 1 corkscrew
- 1 glass per person for each wine
- 1 sheet of paper marked with the wine letters
- 2 plastic cups per person—one for water, one to act as a spittoon
- paper and pencils
- large carafe of water or sparkling mineral water
- water biscuits or bread (optional)
- tissues or paper napkins
- receptacle for collecting waste wine

spoil it. Invest in a wire or wooden rack, don't leave the bottles in the carton. The dividing walls will soon give way when the carton is turned on its side.

If you can, store the wine in a dark spot at an even 54° F/12° C. If this is not possible, concentrate on finding an area with a consistent temperature. Wine suffers more from fluctuations in temperature than from being stored at a few degrees above or below the ideal temperature.

Few people own a wine cellar these days, but it is usually possible to find a suitable spot to keep your wine. Ideas include a chest of drawers in a spare room, or a recess under the stairs. The temperature in the garage will probably fluctuate too much, but this can be solved by insulating the bottles in an unused refrigerator or freezer.

Many people have to keep their wine racks in the living room or kitchen. If you are one of them, place the rack as far away as possible from any heat source and remember that this includes the refrigerator as well as the stove or fireplace.

SETTING UP THE TASTING

Organizing a tasting is very straightforward. Begin by setting out as many glasses for each person as there are wines. Most of the tastings in the book feature six wines; if you do not have enough glasses to accommodate larger groups, ask everyone to bring their own.

If you still do not have enough glasses you may be able to use the same glass for more than one tasting. However, you will need to clear the glass of the first wine before moving on to the second. The method adopted by the professionals—and by far the simplest—is to rinse out the glass you are using with the next wine to be tasted.

It is a good idea to mark large sheets of white paper with a labeled position for each glass. This will help you to remember which wine is which and should keep you from mixing them up.

Make sure that everyone has plenty of paper on which to write rough notes. If you have time you might make a list of all the wines in the tasting. Include information from the label such as wine-growing region, appellation, grower or *négociant*, grape variety, and any vintage.

Choose a corkscrew with a curved end; those with straight ends may cause small pieces of cork to fall into the wine. (This is unsightly but it does not affect the wine. Simply scoop it out.)

Add pencils to your checklist and tissues or paper napkins for wiping the base of glasses. Serve water (still or sparkling) and, if you wish, water biscuits or bread for clearing the palate between wines. Do not serve cheese or other foods as they tend to confuse the tastebuds.

During a tasting session you can consume much more wine than you realize. After a time the alcohol in the wine will start to affect your judgment and this is why the experts spit between every wine. The best way to organize spittoons at home is to provide everyone with their own plastic cup that can be emptied from time to time.

Even though you should pour only a small amount into the glass, there is likely to be some wine left in the glass after tasting. Provide a large bowl or jug into which tasters can empty their glasses.

LABELING THE GLASSES AVOIDS CONFUSION

SERVING THE WINE

To open a bottle of still wine (as opposed to sparkling wine such as Champagne), remove the foil capsule and wipe the top of the bottle. Insert the corkscrew and pull the cork. You may need to wipe around the rim of the bottle again.

Apart from some very expensive red Bordeaux or port, you do not need to decant wine. Red wine used to be decanted in the days when all red wines threw a sediment in the bottom of the bottle. Today, a great deal of wine is filtered and made to be drunk within a few years and no sediment is formed.

You may also hear people say that they wish to let the wine "breathe" for a while before serving it. Opening a bottle and leaving it to stand is thought to allow the wine to take up oxygen and so age quickly. In fact, the amount of air that gets to the wine is minimal and will not make a great deal of difference.

A young wine from a classic area such as Bordeaux, Tuscany, Rioja, or the Napa Valley might benefit from a little air, though there are many who say the glass is decanter enough. However, this could be a good opportunity to show off your best decanter and the transfer from bottle to decanter will give the wine more air than simply removing the cork. Do not decant if you have any reason to think that the wine is past its prime—the air will just make it worse.

Wine tastes best when served at the correct temperature. If you have ever tasted a bottle of unchilled white wine you will know that it can taste unpleasantly fulsome and may seem flat or cloying. Correctly chilled wine tastes lighter, fresher and fruitier, but wine that has been over-chilled loses much of its flavor. This, of course, can be useful if you have bought an indifferent bottle of wine.

The recommendation used to be to serve red wine at room temperature and white wine at cellar temperature. This was probably useful when the average wine-drinker owned a cellar and central heating was unknown. Better advice today is to serve red wine at about 62° F/16° C—which is a little cooler than the average living room—and white wine at about 50°F/10°C—which will be reached after about an hour in the refrigerator.

The best way to chill wine if you are in a hurry is to use a ice bucket. Fill it with ice cubes and water, rather than ice alone, and push the bottle in as deeply as it will go. The wine will chill in about 15 to 20 minutes. This is a much quicker way of achieving the correct temperature than placing the bottle in the freezer. This method can also be used to cool down red wine that is too warm. Allow about five minutes in this case.

An alternative is to invest in a special bag that is kept in the freezer for use whenever you need to chill a bottle quickly. It will chill a bottle of white wine in just five minutes and will keep it cool for hours.

CHOOSING THE GLASSES

Just as the temperature of a wine affects your appreciation of it, so too does the glass from which you drink. A good tasting glass is made of clear glass so that you can view its contents easily. Cut and colored glasses may look good but tend to obscure what they hold.

Make sure that the glass has a stem long enough to offer a comfortable grip without your hand touching the bowl, and a foot wide enough to give a firm base. The bowl should funnel gently inwards, helping to channel the aroma of the wine to your nose. Avoid glasses that curve out at the top. If you like, you can buy glasses that have been specifically designed for tasting. They are known as INAO glasses.

Carefully wash and dry your glasses before use. If detergent or powder is left on the glass it will affect the taste, and will stir up the bubbles in sparkling wine. Water left in the glass will dilute the wine. Lastly, do not leave the glasses in the carton between tastings or they will begin to smell of cardboard.

Using the Leftovers

If you do not finish a bottle of wine during your tasting you can simply re-cork it to drink later in the day. The best way to seal the wine is to invest in a bottle stopper that works by removing the air from the bottle. Some use a vacuum pump with rubber stoppers; others replace the air with gas. Wine closed in this way will keep for a week or two.

The choice of stopper is yours, but bear in mind that rubber stoppers eventually split and need to be replaced, and gas canisters must be stored in cool conditions. Sparkling wine requires its own special type of stopper; the air and gas methods are not suitable here.

How to Taste Wine

To taste wine all you need are your own senses of sight, smell and taste—plus a little practice. After all, you can easily tell the difference between pineapples and strawberries. It is simply a matter of adding to the taste memory you already have by making a conscious effort to notice the different aromas and flavors of each wine as you taste it.

A great many people just lift the glass to their lips and drink without thinking about how the wine smells. They will, of course, get some taste of the wine and, indeed, will be able to decide whether they like it or not. But there is a great deal more to assessing a wine than this.

Flavor is actually a reflection of both smell and taste with the emphasis on the sense of smell, so you need to use both your nose and your tastebuds and to make a mental and written note of what they are telling you. In this way you will eventually train your memory to remember the differences.

Next time you have a glass of wine, hold your nose with your finger and thumb while you take a

---

Correct Serving Temperatures for Wine

Use the guidelines below to determine the temperature at which your wine should ideally be served:

- Mature red wines 60°- 64°F / 15°- 17°C
- Young red wines and country wines, such as French Vin de Pays wines 56°- 58°F / 13°-14°C
- Very light red wines such as Beaujolais 52°F / 11°C
- Champagne and dry white wine 48°- 50°F / 9°- 10°C
- Sweet white wines 45°F / 7°C

mouthful and swallow. See how much of the wine you can taste. Contrast this with a mouthful taken normally. You will see from this experiment just how important your sense of smell is in tasting wine.

Your tongue is able to detect just four primary tastes—sweet, salt, sour and bitter—and tastebuds on different parts of the tongue are sensitive to particular tastes. Thus sweet and salty foods are tasted at the tip of the tongue and sour foods in the middle. The tastebuds that detect bitterness are situated at the back of the tongue and are activated only on swallowing.

APPEARANCE AND COLOR

Wine-tasting starts with a look at the color and appearance of the wine. Check that the glass is clean by giving it a good sniff before pouring the wine. It should smell of nothing at all. Pour a small amount of the wine into the glass, so that the bowl is about a quarter full.

Hold the glass against a white background and look at the wine. What you see can tell you something about the age of the wine and where it might have come from. It may also indicate a fault in the wine.

NOSE

The second step is to smell the wine. The bouquet or aroma that comes off the wine is known to professional tasters as the "nose." The best way to assess the nose is to hold the glass firmly by the stem and swirl the wine in the bowl. The swirling action is important as it adds a little oxygen to the wine and helps to release all the aromas. Place your nose close to the glass and take a good sniff.

What do these aromas remind you of? First impressions are vital so it is important to make a note immediately. It does not matter how odd your comparisons may seem. They are based on your personal experience and are the building blocks for your own taste memory.

PALATE

The third step is to taste the wine to see if your palate confirms the analysis you have made on the nose. Is the wine as fresh and fruity as you thought it was on the nose, or is it rather disappointing?

Tasting the wine will also tell you how sweet or dry it is and how much acidity and tannin is present. Acidity gives the wine a sharp, sometimes astringent taste, and tannin gives it a kind of "furry" feel. Your palate will tell you if the wine is balanced, with all these components in harmony—a sign of a good wine. All these factors have tastings devoted to them later in the book and there is advice on the kind of notes to make.

To experience all the attributes of a wine you must make sure that the wine is rolled all round the mouth and over the entire surface of the tongue. A very small quantity of the wine will naturally be swallowed. This enables the bitterness tastebuds to come into play. The rest of the wine is spit out.

Expert tasters try to take in a little air with the wine, using their teeth to form a barrier as they suck air in though the gaps. This can be quite difficult at first but it is worth practicing in private as the air helps to bring out the flavors of the wine. Do not worry about the noise you will inevitably make—the professionals don't.

Finally, add a further note to those you have already made on the palate on the tastes and flavors that remain in the mouth after you have spit out the wine. This is known as the "finish." A long finish is one where the flavors linger in the mouth for a minute or more. This adds to the enjoyment of the wine and is a sign of quality. Conversely, a lesser wine will have a short finish or may have no finish at all.

CONCLUSIONS

Using your notes on the color, nose and palate of the wine, make an overall assessment of the wine. This is your chance to sum up the wine in a way that will be useful to you in the future.

It can be helpful to invent a mnemonic to help you remember each component. The way to do this is to take the first letter of each of the key words and to make up of a sentence from them.

On the nose the elements include:

C	cleanliness or lack of faults
G	grape variety
F	fruitiness
I	intensity
W	wood
M	maturity

On the palate the elements include:

F	flavors (overall impression of fruit and wood)
S	sweetness/dryness
A	acidity
T	tannin
B	body or mouthfeel
B	balance
F	finish

Your mnemonic for the nose could be something like Cats Get Frightened In Wet Months. For the palate it could be Find Some Apples To Bring Back Fred—it does not matter so long as it helps you to remember!

Keep your notes short and to the point and make them quickly. Don't wait to think about them for too long—your all-important first impressions will have disappeared. Use whichever words pop into your head; they will be the basis for your own taste memory. All kinds of words are used to describe wine. Those that attempt to give a general description of what is in the bottle such as "fruity," "flowery," "rich," "mature," and "body" are generally accepted. So are some fruit comparisons such as "black currant," "strawberry," "cherry," and "gooseberry."

Of course, the wine does not actually smell or taste exactly like the description, but is reminiscent of it. However, everyone's perception differs and one person's "cherry" may be another person's "plum" or just "ripe fruit."

Some professional tasters revel in phrases such as "sweaty leather," or "farmyard manure," and if these comparisons appeal to you by all means use them. If they do not, you can opt for a simpler description.

You will, of course, learn more about the sort of things to note and the accepted descriptions for them as you progress through the book. There is also a glossary and a brief description of how grapes are grown and how wine is made.

ASSESSING THE CLUES

Most people can tell good wine from bad wine. Good wine tastes wonderful and bad wine just tastes unpleasant. Nor is it too difficult to grade the everyday wines that fall in between.

Even though you may not know a great deal about wine, you probably know more than you think you do. You certainly know which wines you like and which you do not. What you may not be able to do is to explain exactly why a wine is good or bad or convey why you like the wines that you do.

The clues are all in the bottle. They lie in the appearance and color of the wine, its aroma or "nose," its initial flavors, and its aftertaste or "finish." A detailed assessment of these clues will give you more than enough information to make discerning judgments that can be expressed to other people.

Looking at wine in this way can also give you a great deal of extra enjoyment. With practice, you will be able to decide whether a wine is too young, whether it is ready to drink, or whether it is "going over the hill." You will also find it easier to choose wines to go with your favorite foods.

By keeping notes on the wines as you taste them, you will have an invaluable record to which you can refer in the future.

APPEARANCE IN WHITE WINE

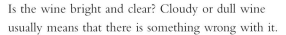 Pour the white wine. Hold the glass against a sheet of white paper and tip the glass slightly so that you get a better view of the surface of the wine.

THE WINES

A. YOUR FAVORITE WHITE WINE

B. YOUR FAVORITE RED WINE

Is the wine bright and clear? Cloudy or dull wine usually means that there is something wrong with it.

Depending upon which wine you have chosen, you may see some very tiny bubbles attached to the side of the glass or around the rim of the surface of the wine. Muscadet-sur-Lie, for example, often shows this phenomenon. There is nothing wrong with the wine. The bubbles simply show the presence of a little residual carbon dioxide created during fermentation or absorbed during storage from a protective carbon dioxide shield.

EIGHT STEPS TO TASTING WINE

1. Check the glass for any unpleasant smells
2. Pour a small amount of wine into the glass
3. Check the appearance and color of the wine
4. Swirl the wine in the glass
5. Take a deep sniff of the wine and write a descriptive note
6. Take a mouthful of wine and roll it around in your mouth
7. Spit out the wine and write a descriptive note
8. Consider the finish of the wine and complete your notes

Occasionally a white wine will have a few clear crystals at the bottom of the bottle. This is not a flaw. It can occur if the wine has been kept for any length of time in a very cold place. The crystals are made up of tartaric acid, which is naturally present in the grape juice, and that precipitates out of the wine when the temperature is very low. It shows that the wine has not been over-filtered to the extent that it might lose some of its flavor.

Look at the color of the wine. How would you describe it? Try to put a specific color on it such as straw, pale yellow, greenish yellow, buttercup, or golden.

Color in white wine can tell you something about the age of the wine and where it comes from. Most European white wines tend to be pale straw, pale yellow or greenish yellow when they are young. These colors intensify as the wine ages, and by the time a deep golden color is reached most wines will be too old to drink. Important exceptions are the French wines of Burgundy and Sauternes and German wines at the Auslese level and above. These are outlined in Tasting 2.

On the other hand, wine from California, the Pacific Northwest, Australia, Chile and other parts of the new world, usually start off with much more intense buttercup yellow colors and may even be deep golden in color when they are only a year old. This may seem confusing, but with practice your nose will soon tell you whether the wine is from one of the newer wine-making regions, or is one of the above exceptions.

Your nose will also warn you about the final category of deeply colored white wines: those that are oxidized or maderized. These terms refer to wine that has been spoiled by air penetrating the cork.

As well as having a peculiarly dark color, oxidized wine has a rather flat caramel or bad sherry-like aroma. It is, of course, impossible to direct you to a wine that exhibits this fault, but wines that have been stored upright for too long often show it.

APPEARANCE IN RED WINE

Pour the red wine. Hold the glass against a sheet of white paper and tip the glass slightly so that you get a better view of the surface of the wine. Check that the wine is bright and clear.

Now look at the color of the wine. How would you describe it? Try to put a specific color on it such as purple, plum, cherry red, bright red, brick, brownish red or mahogany. How would you gauge the depth of color?

The color of red wine does not tell you as much about its origins as the color of white wine can, but the depth of color in red wine may give you a clue.

Wines such as Cahors from France and mature Shiraz from the Hunter Valley in Australia exhibit particularly deep, almost impenetrable colors. However, well-made wines from the top wine-producing estates of the world will also show this depth of color. It points to two crucial components of first-class wine— good fruit extract and therefore good flavor and high tannin levels. The tannin acts as a general preservative and this is important if the wine is to be kept for any length of time.

Very pale colors point either to bad practice in the vineyard or winery, or to bad weather. Whatever the cause, the wine will taste thin and not very fruity. The red wines of Burgundy are the exception to this rule. Except for the very best examples, burgundies are often fairly pale in color.

Have another look at the color of the wine. Does it have a brownish tinge? If the red colors are still fairly strong, tip the wine in the glass and look at the rim of the wine.

LEGS

Some wines, such as those with a naturally high glycerine content form "legs." These are caused by drops of wine that tail down the sides of the glass after the wine has been swirled in the glass. Some people consider legs to be an indication that the wine will be full-bodied and luscious.

However, some disreputable winemakers add glycerine to the wine illegally to achieve just this effect. Also, carelessly washed or dried glasses can affect the physical behavior of the wine in the glass. It is probably better to rely on your nose and palate rather than your eyes to detect real richness.

Color in red wine can tell you a great deal about the age of the wine and its level of maturity. The first hint of orange or brown on the rim is often an indication that a red wine is reaching its prime. Unlike white wine, which gains in color as it ages, red wine loses color. It fades from the reds and purples, which are typical of young wine, through red brick colors to quite dark brownish reds. Do take care not to confuse a pale red color with a faded color. The latter always tends to shades of brown.

Darkening of red wine can also be caused by air getting into the bottle and oxidizing the wine. This can happen if the cork dries out or if an opened bottle is not sealed with an airtight stopper.

Smell in White Wine

A trained nose can tell the taster almost everything about a wine. Whatever your expertise your nose will immediately tell you whether the wine is "off" or not. It will also tell you something about the grapes the wine was made from, how it was matured, the age of the wine and its complexity.

Return to the white wine you poured earlier. Swirl the wine round the bowl of the glass and have a good sniff. Are there any unpleasant smells coming off the wine?

There are some faults in wine which, once encountered, you are unlikely to forget. One of these is "corked" wine. This term does not refer to wine that has pieces of cork floating in it. It refers to wine that has an unpleasant musty, mushroomy aroma caused by a fungal infection in the cork. The smell is transferred to the wine, and the longer the bottle remains open, the stronger the smell becomes. Other significant problems can also be divined by smell: Can you detect the bad sherry-like aroma of oxidized wine? Is there a smell of vinegar?

A very fleeting smell that you might encounter just as the bottle is opened is sulfur. Some wines are stored under a blanket of sulfur and a little may get caught in the neck of the bottle. When the cork is drawn, the sulfur escapes into the air.

Sulfur is detectable as the kind of acrid smell given off when a match is struck. Some people are not particularly sensitive to this smell and may not notice it. Others are sensitive and the smell can make them cough. There are is usually nothing at all wrong with the wine.

Another smell you might encounter is known as "bottle stink." This is reminiscent of the smell of bad eggs and is caused by the production of hydrogen sulfide and other compounds in the anaerobic conditions of the bottle. It disappears as soon as the air gets to the wine.

You can distinguish between bottle stink and corked or oxidized wines by the fact that the latter two conditions get worse as the wine is poured, whereas bottle stink disappears.

Because your nose can read all of these clues there is no need to taste a wine you have ordered in a restaurant. Simply take a deep sniff, check it for faults, and then either accept or reject the wine. Once you have decided that the wine is fit to drink, you can start to think about what the nose is telling you about the way the wine was made and matured.

Take another sniff of the wine. How would you describe the aromas and how strong are they? Note your reactions at once—if you try to think too long about it, you may lose your first impressions. Closing your eyes may help you concentrate.

What do the aromas remind you of? Did you think of fruits like apples, lemons, bananas, pineapple or tropical fruit, or did words such as mint, herbs, grass or asparagus come to mind?

Certain grape varieties have characteristic aromas and, though these may vary from wine to wine, they are often easily recognizable. Wine made from Sauvignon Blanc, for example, is regularly described as having a gooseberry or tart fruit aroma, sometimes with herbaceous or minty overtones. Wine made from the Muscat grape is often described as grapey. In Tasting 3 you will learn more about what to expect from different white grape varieties.

The white wines of California, Australia and New Zealand, and to some extent those of Chile and South Africa, tend to have much stronger aromas than European wines. They are often described with reference to tropical fruits such as pineapple, guava and melons.

These descriptions are commonly used as a kind of shorthand by wine writers, but they are not etched in stone. In time you will build up an idea of what the experts mean by them, but if you think that the aromas resemble something else, use those words instead.

Do not worry if you are sometimes unable to come up with very specific descriptions. It may be that your chosen wine is not particularly distinctive and you may only be able to describe it rather loosely as fruity or even just as "vinous." The latter simply means smelling of wine.

Many of the world's everyday wines are produced in huge cold-fermentation tanks that are designed to prevent the temperature of the fermenting wine from rising too high. This certainly prevents the production of the kind of tired wines with no zest to them that used to come from some of the warmer wine-growing regions. But it also means that many wines have little in the way of individual fruity flavors and aromas. At best they have a kind of hard candy smell.

Look at the notes you have made on the nose of your white wine. Did you find "vanilla," "toast," "green apples," "lemons," or "honey" among the aromas?

A vanilla aroma is typical of wines that have been matured in new oak barrels. Some wines also smell of toasted bread. In Tasting 4 you will have a chance to taste wines that have been aged in wood.

If your chosen wine is an old-style white Rioja or a heavily oaked California Chardonnay you should certainly be able to detect vanilla. However, you may well have chosen an un-oaked wine and will find none of these aromas.

The aromas on the nose can also give you an indication of the age of the wine. Young wines tend to give off strong, raw smells because their different elements have had little time to settle down and marry or blend together in the bottle. A green apple smell, for example, is often indicative of young white wine. Older wines tend to have a more honeyed style.

SMELL IN RED WINE

Return to the red wine that you poured earlier. Swirl the wine in the bowl of the glass and take a good sniff. Does it smell fit to drink?

Red wines can have the same flaws as white wine so check for oxidation. In red wine this is more likely to result in a "cabbagey" smell. Can you detect the moldy cardboard smell of corked wine? Has it turned to vinegar?

Swirl and sniff again. How would you describe the aromas and how intense are they? Note your reactions at once.

What do the aromas remind you of? Did you think of fruits like raspberries, black currants, plums, red cherries, blueberries or strawberries, or did words such as leaves and stalks, vegetal, earthy, cabbage, pepper or cinnamon spring to mind? Even if the nose does not suggest any specific description at least note whether it is fruity, earthy or vegetal.

Red grape varieties are perhaps even more specific

PINOT NOIR GRAPES

in their aromas than white varieties. Wines based on Cabernet Sauvignon grapes are characteristically described by reference to black currants, though the fruit may seem fresh, raw, baked or reminiscent of jam. Young wines made from Pinot Noir grapes often have a strawberry aroma, while older wines from this variety give off a deep vegetal smell. In Tasting 3 you will have a chance to taste wines made from a number of different red grape varieties.

New world reds are as distinctive as new world whites. Very often they have more fruit extract and are more concentrated than their European counterparts.

Some red wines do not give off very much smell at all. This may be because they are everyday wines which are meant to be drunk with food rather than savored in their own right. If it was a more expensive bottle and it has very little nose, it may be that it is going through a "closed period." This often happens after the first fruity aromas of the young wine have worn off and before the more complex secondary aromas have had a chance to develop in the bottle. Whatever the reason, it may help to swirl the wine in the bowl of your glass another couple of times to release the aromas before sniffing again.

Swirl and sniff again. Do you think the wine has been matured after fermentation in concrete or stainless steel tanks or in wooden casks? Does the wine have any kind of woody aromas, or does it smell of vanilla?

Red wine is more likely than white wine to be matured in wooden casks, but by no means all of it is. Wine that has not "seen" any wood tends to have a less complex and more fruity aroma. So if your wine is full of fruit with no overtones of cedar, woodsmoke or vanilla the chances are that it has not been matured in wooden casks.

Wine that has been matured in this way will take on a variety of different aromas and flavors depending upon the types of casks used. Bordeaux is usually matured in a mixture of old and new wood and its nose is often described as cedarwood. Rioja is aged in new oak barrels and characteristically smells of vanilla.

Some wines spend only a short time in wooden casks, others may be there for a year or more. The type of wood and the time spent in it will affect the nose and taste of a wine. You will have a chance to taste wines matured in a variety of ways in Tasting 4.

OAK CASKS AT CHATEAU MARGAUX

TASTE IN WHITE WINE

Return to the white wine that you poured earlier. Take a mouthful and roll the wine over the full surface of your tongue, drawing in a little air if you can. Is the wine more, or less, fruity than your nose led you to believe? Is it as oaky?

You can now check whether your palate confirms the notes you made on the nose. If you found tropical fruits and vanilla, are these flavors as pronounced on the palate or are they tempered by honey, pepper or lemons?

If, on the other hand, you had difficulty coming up with a precise description of the wine can you now add more to your notes? Even if the flavor is still very light and difficult to describe at least note whether it is pleasant or not. Remember that the more you taste wine the better your descriptive talents will become. A note on the intensity of the flavor, or otherwise, will also be useful.

Repeat the tasting process and make notes on those elements of the wine that did not appear on the nose. Start by thinking about dryness/sweetness levels and acidity.

Deciding how dry or sweet the wine is relatively easy, but your perceptions can be affected by the acidity level of the wine and by its body. The degree of ripe fruitiness can also deceive you into thinking that a wine is sweeter than it really is.

Acidity is often described as tasting of green apples, lemons, citrus fruits or grapefruit. It usually carries an astringent quality with it. Wines that have a low acidity often taste flat or tired. Your perception of acidity may be affected by excess sugar or by the presence of glycerol. You will learn more about all these components in Tasting 2.

Next think about the texture of the wine and how it feels in your mouth. How much body do you think it has?

The body of a wine can vary from very light to extremely full. Body depends upon the depth of fruit extract and the alcoholic content. Sweet white wines, for example, have more body than dry white wines. There is a fuller, more velvety feel to them. Wines with a higher alcoholic content also have more body.

Is the wine in balance or is one component more prominent than all the others?

A balanced wine is one where all the component parts—fruit, sugar, acidity and wood—are in harmony. If one component dominates the others, the wine is not in balance. Sometimes fruit flavors are smothered by excess oak; at others, the different elements seem to stand separately.

Remember that wine is a dynamic thing and the balance of the wine will change over time. A wine that is out of balance when it is young may well develop into an outstanding wine when it is mature. Of course, an everyday wine that is intended to be drunk immediately rather than stored, needs to be in balance from the start.

After you have spit out the wine think about the taste it has left in your mouth. Has it almost disappeared or is it still there?

This taste is known as the "finish" and it too can tell you quite a bit about the wine. In a good wine the pleasant flavors continue from the initial impact in your mouth all the way to the finish. The longer these flavors linger on the palate, the better the wine.

TASTE IN RED WINE

Return to the red wine that you poured earlier. Take a mouthful and roll the wine over the full surface of your tongue, drawing in a little air if you can. Is the wine more, or less, fruity than your nose led you to believe? Is it as oaky?

You can now check whether your palate confirms what you found on the nose. If you found black currants and vanilla, are these flavors as pronounced on the palate or are they tempered by herbaceous flavors, pepper or spices?

If, on the other hand, you had difficulty coming up with a precise description of the wine can you now add more to your notes? Even if the palate still does not suggest any specific description at least make a note as to whether the wine is fruity, earthy or vegetal. A note on the intensity, or otherwise, of the flavors will also be useful.

Repeat the tasting process and make notes on those elements of the wine that did not appear on the nose. Start by thinking about dryness/sweetness levels.

Red wines do not vary nearly as much as white wine in their sweetness levels, but there is an apparent sweetness in some wines from the hotter parts of the world such as central Spain, southern Italy and central Australia. These wines may be quite dry but taste sweeter because of the ripeness of the fruit. Other red wines, such as Lambrusco, really are sweet.

How much acidity do you think is present in the wine?

Young red wines tend to be more acidic than older or mature wines. This acidity gives an astringent quality to the wine that is not as easy to describe as the "apple fresh" or "lemon" acidity of white wine. It is more of a mouth-puckering sensation than an actual flavor. Acidity is important in all wines but particularly in wines that are intended to last for some time. If acidity is low it will disappear before the wine is ready to drink and the wine will be flabby when mature.

Now think about the levels of tannin. How tannic do you think the wine is?

Tannin comes from the skins and seeds of red grapes, which are crushed and fermented along with the juice. If there is a lot of tannin in the wine it can leave your teeth and tongue with a harsh "furry" feeling. There is no tannin in white wine because the skins and seeds are removed before fermentation.

Next think about the texture of the wine and how it feels in your mouth. How much body do you think it has?

Just as in white wine, the body of the wine will give a clue to its level of fruit extract and alcoholic content. A big beefy wine is probably quite high in alcohol and will need some food to partner it. You will learn more about body in wine in Tasting 5.

Is the wine in balance or is one component more prominent than all the others?

Balance in red wine must take in the tannin levels as well as the fruit, sugar, acidity and wood. In young red wines from the classic areas, where wines are expected to mature for a few years before being drunk, the tannins and acidity are exposed and raw. It takes time for these important elements to settle down and marry with the other components of the wine.

If you have chosen a wine of this kind it is worth trying to decide whether you think the fruit will survive until this process is complete and the wine is ready to drink. An indication of the level of fruitiness can often come through on the finish. Of course, this particular bottle will not improve because it has been opened but, if you have more than one bottle or are thinking of buying more, your notes will be a useful guide to the wine's possible development.

If, on the other hand, you have chosen one of the many everyday wines that are made to be drunk within a year or two of the vintage, it should be well balanced from an early stage. Time will not come to the rescue here.

After you have spit out the wine think about the taste it has left in your mouth. Has it almost disappeared or is it still there?

The finish in red wine is as important as in white wine and the longer the finish the better the wine. Some wines that are closed on the nose and harsh in the mouth, with heavy tannins and high acidity have a surprisingly good finish. The prospects for a wine like this are often very good!

CONCLUSIONS

This is your chance to sum up each wine in a way that will be useful to you in the future. Keep the note short and simple. Good examples are "easy-drinking party wine," "mature classic—drink soon," or "distinctive young wine, try in six months."

ACIDITY AND SWEETNESS

One of the first things you are likely to notice when you taste a glass of wine is how sweet or dry it is. Indeed, the descriptions "sweet" and "dry" are among the few that instantly mean something (though not necessarily the same thing) to even the most inexperienced wine drinker. Many wine choices are made on the basis of this attribute alone.

The component in wine that gives the impression of sweetness is, of course, sugar. You detect sugar by the sensations on the tip of the tongue. Sugar adds "body" to a wine (as do alcohol and tannin), making it feel fuller.

White wines, particularly, vary from bone dry to extremely sweet with all shades in between. Red wines tend to be dry, but there is still some variation.

You may already have an idea of how dry or how sweet you like your wines, or you may consider one type of wine more sophisticated than another, but don't be too fixed in your mind until you have tasted the full range.

Grapes contain fruit acids as well as fruit sugars. Acidity gives freshness to a wine. In a good wine the acids and the sugars should balance each other so that the wine tastes neither too acerbic and sour nor too cloyingly sweet.

THE RANGE FROM DRY TO SWEET

Pour wines A, D and E and taste them in that order. Think specifically about how dry or how sweet these wines are and write a short note on each one.

Follow the Eight Steps to Tasting Wine set out at the beginning of Tasting 1. Look for the light bouquet and apple-crisp astringency on the palate of the Muscadet. This is a really dry wine. Most Muscadet is meant to be drunk when it is young, but if you have chosen a wine that is more than a year or two old it may have mellowed a little to give a softer, more honeyed flavor.

Niersteiner Kabinett comes from the Rhine Valley in Germany. Look for flowery, fruity flavors on the nose and palate. This wine will seem much more velvety in texture than the Muscadet. This quality is a sure sign of sweetness in a wine.

THE WINES

A. MUSCADET
from the Loire Valley

B. CHARDONNAY
from California

C. RHINE RIESLING
from Australia

D. NIERSTEINER KABINETT
from the Rheinhessen

E. MOSCATEL DE VALENCIA
from Spain

F. SAUTERNES
from Bordeaux

If you would like to do the optional tasting of Sauternes on page 33, buy two bottles: the most inexpensive bottle you can find and the most expensive you can afford. Remember that you can often buy half bottles of Sauternes.

Moscatel de Valencia is sweeter still. It is made from the Muscat grape, the only variety that actually gives a grapey flavor to the wine. Muscat Canelli is made from the same grape—known as Orange Muscat in California. It, too, has a grapey flavor but is often very flowery.

Which of these wines do you like the best? Do you think that you might like some of the wines on the list that fall in between those used in this initial selection?

Remember that wine is very much a matter of taste. You do not have to like or dislike wines at any particular sweetness level; simply choose those that are right for you. If you normally always buy the same type of wine, you may be surprised by how wide a difference there is between the driest and the sweetest wine in this tasting.

In America, specific sugar levels are often given on the labels of sweet dessert wines, but rarely on other wines. In Europe a taste guide has been devised to help consumers find their way around the sweetness and dryness levels of the many white wines on sale. Although not in use in America, the principle behind the system is a useful one to be aware of. It uses a scale of 1 to 9 to indicate the range from dry to sweet.

Starting at 1, the wines are bone dry. The Muscadet in the tasting falls into this category. At the other end of the scale, wines rated at 9 are very, very sweet dessert wines like Muscat de Beaumes de Venise. Moscatel de Valencia is not quite as sweet as this and is usually rated at level 8. California Muscat Canelli wines vary from medium sweet (4 to 5 on the European scale) to exceedingly sweet.

German Kabinett wines fall in the middle of the range at about 4 to 5. Exceptions are Trocken Kabinett (very dry) and Halbtrocken Kabinett (half dry) wines, which come in at 2 and 3 respectively.

Taste wine E, then wines D and A. How does tasting the wines in this order affect your perception of their sweetness levels?

Wine D will probably not taste quite so sweet now, and wine A will seem very dry indeed. If you like, you could taste a little lemon juice before tasting the Muscadet (wine A) again. The wine will probably not seem quite so dry now! From these simple experiments you will begin to see that it can make a big difference how and when you serve a particular wine.

Your perception of sweetness and dryness depends very much on what you have tasted immediately before. This is why dry wines are usually served before sweet ones and why dry wines do not go very well with sweet desserts.

The Importance of Acidity in Wine

In addition to sugar, grapes contain fruit acids. The amount of fruit acid depends on the grape variety and their degree of ripeness when harvested. Wine made from young fruit will contain much more acidity than

Where Some Popular White Wines Fall on the European 1 to 9 Sweetness Scale

Dry

Chablis (FR) 1
Entre-deux-Mers and dry white Bordeaux (FR) 1
Muscadet (FR) 1
Fumé Blanc (USA) 1
Sancerre (FR) 1
Sauvignon Blanc (FR, USA, CH, AUST, NZ) 1
White Burgundy (FR) 2
Chardonnay (FR, USA, AUST, CH) 2

Medium

Kabinett wines (GER) 4
Vinho Verde (POR) 4
Liebfraumilch (GER) 5

Sweet

Sauternes and Barsac (FR) 8
Moscatel de Valencia (SP) 8
Late Harvest Riesling (USA) 8
Muscat de Beaumes de Venise (FR) ... 9

wine made from over-ripe fruit.

The level of acidity in a wine is as important as the level of sugar, and the two should balance each other. The amount of acidity in a wine can affect your judgment of how sweet or dry it is.

Pour wines B, C and F and line them up with the wines you have already tasted. Now taste the Muscadet (wine A) again, followed by the Chardonnay (wine B). Think about the sweetness/dryness levels. Which wine do you think is the drier of the two and how much difference do you think there is between them?

The Muscadet should be more obviously dry than the Chardonnay, but the difference may seem greater than it is. To some extent this will depend on precisely which wines you have chosen for the tasting, and your answer will not be quite the same if you chose some other wines another time.

However, the chances are that the Chardonnay will give you a much fuller and less strident feeling in the mouth and you may think that this means that it is a lot sweeter. The Chardonnay will also taste much fruitier, but this is a matter of grape variety (see page 35), so try not to let it distract you from considering the sweetness levels.

In fact these two wines are rated at sweetness levels 1 and 2 and so they are not all that different. What may be different is the level of *acidity*.

WINE CLASSIFICATION LAWS BASED ON SUGAR LEVELS

Unlike the other European wine-growing countries, which base the classification of their wines solely on geographical areas; the German and Austrian wine laws are based on both geographical areas and the ripeness or sweetness levels of the grape juice. The riper the grapes the better the wine. The key descriptions are:

Qualitätswein mit Prädikat (QmP)
This is the overall classification for the best German wines. The term QmP will appear on the label together with one of the following categories:
Kabinett: Wine made from grapes picked at the normal time. Sweetness rating 4.

Spätlese: Wine made from late-picked grapes with more flavor. Sweetness rating 5 to 6.
Auslese and Beerenauslese: Wine made from selected and very ripe bunches of late-picked grapes. Sweetness rating 6 to 7.
Trockenbeerenauslese: Wine made from shriveled almost raisin-like grapes. Sweetness rating 8.
Eiswein: Wine made from very ripe grapes which have frozen on the vine. Sweetness rating 7 to 8.

If you liked the German Kabinett wine in the tasting you might like to try a sweetness/dryness tasting using only German wine. Choose a Trocken Kabinett, a dry wine rated 2; a Kabinett wine, rated 4 or 5; and an Auslese at 6 or 7.

MONDAVI WINERY, NAPA VALLEY

Taste wines A and B again and write a note on each wine thinking specifically about the level of acidity present. Do they seem at all sharp or sour like lemon juice or green apples, or are they more soft and gentle?

The clean sharp sensation of acidity is felt on the sides of the tongue. Acidity in wine sometimes tastes rather like lemon or grapefruit juice, at others more like green apples. Over-acidic wines can be quite sour and "acidic" is the correct description.

If you have used words like crisp, zesty or sharp you can be sure that the wine has a high level of

RHINE RIESLING

Rhine Riesling is increasingly being produced in Australia, and more and more of it is finding its way beyond its own shores, although it has not yet achieved the popularity of Australian Chardonnay. It is made from the Rhine Riesling grape, which originated in Germany.

Some of the best Australian Rhine Riesling comes from the Clare Valley in south Australia. Check that the word "Rhine" appears on the label; Clare Riesling is made from the inferior Crouchen grape.

VINEYARD OVERLOOKING NIERSTEIN VILLAGE IN THE RHEINHESSEN

acidity. An attractive level of lemon or citrus acidity gives freshness to a wine and indeed the word "fresh" may spring to mind. Wines with lower levels of acidity are known as "soft." White wines that do not have enough acidity are often described as "flabby," though you will never find this description on a wine list!

Flabby wines are flat and boring. They do not have any "get up and go" to them. Flabby wines may crop up at any sweetness level. It is, of course, impossible to offer a specific example for you to taste, but think of this description when you are tasting all of the wines in this book.

Now taste wine C. What level on the sweetness scale do you think this is? Write a note on this and on the acidity of the wine.

American producers use the Chenin Blanc grape variety to make easy, semi-dry wines for everyday drinking. The best of these (from the north coast of California and Washington State) have quite high acidity levels and as a result often taste drier than they really are.

The Australian Rhine Riesling is a well-flavored Australian wine that offers a mixture of tropical fruit

ACIDITY LEVELS

There are a number of other wines you could have chosen to illustrate the importance of acidity levels.

Gros Plant, is a very dry wine that comes from the mouth of the Loire Valley not far from the Muscadet-producing region of France. Its acidity level is usually so high that it tastes even drier than the Muscadet.

This kind of high acidity is often rather euphemistically described as "crisp," so treat this adjective with caution. Dry white wine is often held up as the sophisticated choice, but there is nothing sophisticated about an over-acidic wine.

Like Australian Rhine Riesling, Vinho Verde wines from northern Portugal are rated at a sweeter level than you might expect from their taste. In fact, they are naturally very acidic wines that are sweetened for export. If they are well balanced they can be very good.

and flowers rather reminiscent of good German wine. It is usually considered to be medium dry and is rated at the 3 or 4 level. However, its acidity level is generally quite high and as a result it can easily be mistaken for a drier wine. It makes a very good aperitif and can be served with a variety of foods.

Now taste the Niersteiner (wine D) again and compare it with the Rhine Riesling (wine C). Do they taste as if they are separated only by one step on the sweetness scale, or do you think the difference is more marked? What do you think about their respective levels of acidity?

Here again the depth of contrast will depend upon the wines you have chosen. Check the sweetness levels from the shelf descriptions in the store, if there are any, and make a note of them so that you can compare your tasting notes with the actual sweetness. For acidity levels you will have to rely on your own tastebuds.

Now taste the remaining two wines, Moscatel de Valencia (wine E) and Sauternes (wine F), in that order.

This time think about the acidity level of the Moscatel de Valencia as well as its sweetness level. The wine is obviously sweet and velvety, but you are not left with a cloying sensation in the mouth. In fact, the finish is very fresh and clean. This is because the acidity in the wine balances the sugar and you are left with a pleasant feeling in the mouth.

Your reaction to the Sauternes will probably

depend upon how much you have spent on it. Good Sauternes is very expensive to produce and the chances are that a wine at a lower price will not have enough acidity to balance the sweetness.

The result is a rather unpleasant sweetly cloying feeling in the mouth after you have tasted the wine. Contrast this with the clean and fresh taste left by the Moscatel. Of course, you may strike lucky and come up with a good Sauternes. If so, sit and enjoy it at the end of your meal.

WHY WINES VARY IN THEIR SWEETNESS AND ACIDITY LEVELS

The reasons for these variations are many. Some grape varieties, such as Sémillon (used to make Sauternes) and Muscat (used to make Moscatel), simply contain more natural sugar than others and so yield a sweeter

juice or "must" than other varieties. Grapes also vary in their acidity levels, some varieties being naturally much more acidic than others.

The timing of the harvest is another very important factor. As grapes ripen, their sugar content increases and their acid content drops. In cooler countries, such as Germany, the grapes may never reach their full sweetness potential. In hot areas, such as central Spain and southern Italy, they can easily over-ripen and start to lose acidity.

When the grape must is fermented, yeasts are added to the mix to convert the natural sugar to alcohol. In theory fermentation stops when all the sugar has been used up, but if the must is very sweet alcohol levels can become very high. When they reach a concentration of 14 to 15 percent the yeasts die off, leaving a residue of natural sugar in the wine.

Unlike sugar, fruit acids are not affected by the fermentation process and remain in the wine. It is the winemaker's job to adjust the acid and sugar levels in the fermenting must to achieve a balanced wine. This is why German winemakers add grape juice (Süsswein) to sweeten some of their wines and others add citric acid or gypsum to increase the acidity.

SWEETNESS AND ACIDITY IN RED WINE

By and large red wines do not vary nearly as much in their sweetness levels as white wines. There are a few sweet red wines, such as Lambrusco from central Italy and sparkling Shiraz from Australia, but they are not the norm. Most red wines are medium dry to dry.

However, acidity is just as important in red wine as it is in white wine—a flabby red is just as unpleasant

---

TERMS MEANING SWEET AND DRY

FRENCH:	ITALIAN:
Brut: This means dry, but it does not always indicate quite the same degree of dryness.	Amaro: Bitter
	Secco: Dry
	Abbocato: Semi-sweet
	Dolce: Sweet
Sec: Should mean dry, but often merely means medium dry	GERMAN:
	Trocken: Dry
Demi-sec: Usually means fairly sweet	Halbtrocken: Medium dry
Doux: Sweet	

as a flabby white. Acidity gives a wine zest and life. It does not manifest itself in quite the same fruity guise as in white wine, but it can be just as searing on the palate if there is too much of it.

Descriptions for red wine tend to concentrate on the degree of acidity such as light, medium or strong, though you will find that words like "fresh" and "flabby" are used here too. If you would like to set up a tasting on acidity in red wine choose a wine from northern Italy such as Barbera d'Alba, a good

Bordeaux, and a Cabernet Sauvignon from California or Australia. This should give you a good range from highly acidic to soft and rich.

🍷 Complete the tasting by checking through your mnemonic, making full notes on the color, nose and palate of each wine. On the nose use your mnemonic for CGFIWM. On the palate remember FSATBBF. Transfer your notes to the notebook.

Optional tasting of dessert wines

These wines are both very sweet. They are part of the group of wines known as dessert wines because they complement these foods so well. In America a "dessert wine" is defined legally by an alcohol content of between 15 and 22 percent. In Europe these wines are known as fortified wines. The best sweet wines have a wonderful depth of flavor that is very sophisticated and quite unique.

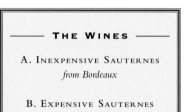

THE WINES

A. INEXPENSIVE SAUTERNES
from Bordeaux

B. EXPENSIVE SAUTERNES
from Bordeaux

🍷 Do you think that either of the wines has any kind of distinctive taste?

You will probably find that not only do the wines vary in their acidity levels but that they also taste very different. Look for a wonderful caramel taste mixed with the flavor of dried raisins or apricots. This is typical of wine made from grapes that have been affected by a fungus known as botrytis cinerea.

🍷 Pour wines A and B and taste them in that order. Which do you like the best?

Unless you have been very lucky, the acidity level in the inexpensive Sauternes will probably not be very high. This means that you will get the kind of unpleasant cloying sensation outlined above. Compare this to the clean acidity of the more costly Sauternes.

Normally an attack by mold is a disaster in the vineyard because it causes the grapes to rot and fall off the vine. In the case of botrytis cinerea things are very different. Wine made from grapes that have been attacked by botrytis develop a wonderful raisin-like flavor which really enhances the wine. It was in appreciation of this that growers rechristened the mold "noble rot."

NOBLE ROT

If you like the taste of wines affected by noble rot try Barsac, which is very similar to Sauternes, or German Trockenbeerenauslese wines. A more economical buy might be a Premières Côtes de Bordeaux. Some châteaux in this less well-known region of Bordeaux, such as Château de Berbec, produce very good sweet wines, which in the best years are affected by noble rot.

Noble rot rarely occurs

naturally in the United States, but Californian growers have pioneered a method of spraying the mold onto the grapes. The Australians have followed suit. These wines are usually labeled late harvest, late-picked, late-select harvest or even botrytis-affected. Particularly good examples are Johannisberg Riesling from California and the Muscat and Riesling wines of north-east Victoria in Australia.

The very best Sauternes are made from grapes that are left on the vine until they are extremely ripe. In certain years they are attacked by botrytis cinerea, and with luck your Sauternes will have been affected in this way.

Dessert wines like these are the result of fermentation stopping before all the sugar in the wine has turned to alcohol. This may occur naturally but is more usually achieved artificially by the winemaker killing off the yeasts either with sulfur or by adding more alcohol in the form of grape brandy. The latter will result in a fortified wine (see Tasting 5).

Catching a sweet wine at just the right stage of fermentation can be a tricky business. Add to this the uncertainty of the appearance of noble rot in the vineyards, and the difficulty of selecting and picking the affected grapes by hand, and you will have some idea of why these wines are so expensive.

When botrytis cinerea attacks red grapes the result is not usually so pleasing. However, in northern Italy grapes that are being dried to make Amarone and Recioto della Valpolicella (see page 45) are sometimes attacked by the mold. Some producers welcome the extra dimension given to the flavor of their wine. Others try to avoid it by spraying the vines.

FRUIT FLAVORS

All the fruity flavors in a wine come from the grape "must" or juice, so it is the grape variety that provides the basic flavor of a wine. Some grape varieties such as Gewürztraminer yield very fruity wines indeed, while others like Trebbiano only offer light fruit.

"Fruity" is one of the most over-worked words in wine-tasting. Yet, it is often the only description suitable for the many wines that have very fruity aromas and flavors, but which are not reminiscent of any specific fruit.

Some wines, of course, do have very definite aromas that conjure up flavor memories of actual fruits such as melons, strawberries, black currants or lychees. You might expect this list to include grapes and some wines, such as those made from the Muscat grape, do indeed taste like dessert grapes, but most wines do not.

Descriptive comparisons with the flavor of other fruits is not as far-fetched as it might seem. Research has shown that there are chemical compounds in some wines that correspond to those found in the fruit to which they are most often compared. For example, the pineapple flavors often detected in young new world Chardonnay wines comes from the presence of ethyl caprylate, which is also found in pineapples.

Some wines are very pleasantly fruity but do not have a great deal of *depth*. Others have very concentrated fruit flavors. This depth of fruit extract is affected by both the climate and the decisions made by the winemaker.

Wines from hot countries are likely to be made from grapes that are very much riper than those grown in cooler climates and so will yield more fruit extract. In some areas, winemakers may choose to use special production methods—such as carbonic maceration, extended exposure to the skins, or fermentation on the lees—to increase fruitiness.

What fruit extract there is in a wine changes over time. Thus the way that the wine has been matured and its age will also affect its flavor. Wines that have been aged for a very long time, whether in wood or in the bottle, lose their fresh fruity flavors. If they are designed to last they take on more complex flavors, if not they just fade away, losing all fruitiness.

This tasting concentrates on fruit extract and fruity flavors in wine. Follow the Eight Steps to Tasting Wine set out at the beginning of Tasting 1.

THE WINES

A. SOAVE
from Italy

B. SAUVIGNON DE TOURAINE
from France, or
New Zealand Sauvignon Blanc

C. GEWÜRZTRAMINER
from anywhere

D. RED BURGUNDY
from France

E. CABERNET SAUVIGNON
from California, Chile, Bulgaria
or Australia

F. CROZES-HERMITAGE
from France

FRUIT IN WHITE WINE

Pour wines A, B and C. Begin by tasting wine A. Think about how fruity it is and write a note on the aromas and flavors you find.

Soave is made from the Trebbiano and Garganega grape varieties and these are not known for their full fruitiness. However, if they are handled carefully they can produce wine that has a definite fruity quality. You may find that your Soave can only be described as vinous, and even if you decide that it is quite fruity you are unlikely to be able to write down a specific fruit comparison.

Italian wines have traditionally been made to drink with food, and the idea that wine should be flavorsome in its own right was foreign to Italian winemakers. However, things are beginning to change and some producers of white wine are experimenting with new methods. Instead of immediately separating the "must" or grape juice from the skins and pips in the usual way, these producers are leaving it in contact with the skins for a while. This results in much more flavor but little more color because green grapes, unlike red ones, do not have very much color in their skins.

THE CASTLE OF SOAVE, IN THE VENETO

Now taste wine B. Think about how fruity it is and write a note on the aromas and flavors you find. How does it compare with wine A?

Sauvignon Blanc is one of those grape varieties on which there is some consensus. The gooseberry is the fruit to which wine made from this grape is most often compared. But, descriptions such as minty and catnip, or simply herbaceous are also very common. What do you think about your sample?

If you have chosen a French Sauvignon de Touraine you may well agree with the gooseberry description. Some of these wines immediately suggest gooseberry pie, others are sharper and smell more of the raw fruit. If your Sauvignon Blanc is from New Zealand you may decide that catnip is the best comparison. Alternatively, you may think of words like grassy or leafy. There is no correct answer.

Whatever the description you give to your sample of Sauvignon Blanc, you must also think about the depth or intensity of the fruit extract. Some wines have quite definite fruit flavors that are easy to describe, but not always very intense. Others are very strong indeed.

Taste wine C. Think about how fruity it is and write a note on the aromas and flavors you find. How does it compare with A and B?

The Gewürztraminer grape produces a very definite wine, which is probably one of the fruitiest in the world. Most people either love it or hate it. Its flavor is often compared to lychees, but it is such a complex wine that you may detect many different aromas that you would not necessarily compare to fruit.

Some Gewürztraminer wines are very spicy; others are much more flowery. These differences are as much due to the different production methods used by the winemaker as to where the wine originates.

Gewürztraminer is best known for its wines from Alsace in France and from Germany. Alsace is one of the few regions of France that labels most of its wines by grape variety rather than by estate or vineyard. Gewürztraminer is also being produced with a good deal of success in Oregon and Washington State, in New Zealand, and in eastern Europe.

Turn back to the notes you made on three of the white wines sampled in Tasting 2: the **Chardonnay (wine B)**, the **Rhine Riesling (wine C)** and the **Moscatel de Valencia (wine E)**.

Chardonnay from California, Chile, Australia and New Zealand is nearly always full of ripe fruity aromas and flavors. Melons, pineapples, guavas and tropical fruits are the descriptive comparisons most used.

HIDDEN GRAPE VARIETIES

French wines made from Sauvignon Blanc. include Sancerre and Pouilly-Fumé, and the lesser known Quincy and Ménétou-Salon. A number of white wines from Bordeaux also use this grape variety. In America some Sauvignon Blanc wines are labeled Fumé Blanc.

If you like wines made from this grape, you might set up another tasting using wines A and B, a Sancerre, a Bordeaux Sauvignon and a California Fumé Blanc.

In contrast, a European Chardonnay may be much lighter in flavor, and comparisons with hard candy and honey are common. Surprisingly, there are some Chardonnay wines that have very little varietal character at all.

The Rhine Riesling, too, has plenty of tropical fruit flavor, though you might not have been quite so specific in your descriptions. The Moscatel is one of those few wines that actually taste of grapes.

WHITE GRAPE FLAVORS

A number of fruit flavors are associated with particular white grape varieties. Not all wines made from these grape varieties will exhibit the flavors listed, but many will:

Apple: Chardonnay, Muscadet
Apricot: Viognier
Gooseberry: Sauvignon Blanc or Fumé Blanc
Grapes: Muscat and Moscatel

Grapefruit: Young Riesling
Lemon: Young Sémillon
Lychee: Gewürztraminer
Mango: Chardonnay
Melon: Sémillon, Chardonnay
Peach: Sémillon
Pineapple: New world Chardonnay, Sémillon
Tropical fruits: Australian Chardonnay and Sémillon

FRUIT IN RED WINE

Pour wines D, E and F. Begin by tasting wine D. Think about how fruity it is and write a note on the aromas and flavors you find.

With the exception of Beaujolais and a wine called Passe-Tout-Grains, all red wines from Burgundy are made from the Pinot Noir grape. Very young Pinot Noir tends to smell quite different from the mature wine, and usually has masses of ripe strawberry and raspberry flavors.

As it matures, the wine takes on a much more vegetal aroma and flavor that has been described as "farmyardy," "cheesey manure" and even "old socks." Some tasters maintain that cooked beet is the definitive aroma of Pinot Noir.

When the wine is between these two stages it often goes into a closed phase, giving off very little aroma indeed.

Depending on your red Burgundy's age, origin, and price it might have any of the aromas described. Check these facts from the label and add them to your notes. When you read them again in the future you will be able to see to what kind of wine your description refers.

The simple red wines of Burgundy such as Bourgogne (the French name for Burgundy), Hautes Côtes de Nuit and Hautes Côtes de Beaune will be ready to drink within two or three years. They will not have the same depth of fruit extract as those from more important areas such as Corton and Pommard which need many years to reach full maturity. Nuits St-Georges falls somewhere in the middle.

In practice it is very difficult to predict how the contents of a bottle of red Burgundy will taste unless you know the producer well. Many of the great vineyards have been broken up into myriads of small plots. Some owners are part of well-established wine-making companies; others are one-man bands. Two wines may be labeled in the same way, for example Corton or Nuits St-Georges, but one might be very much better than the other.

The Pinot Noir grape offers something of a challenge to winemakers around the world, as the variety does not really like conditions outside its native Burgundy. However, it is grown quite successfully in the cooler parts of the Sonoma and Napa Valleys around Carneros, and in Monterey in California; in Oregon and Idaho; in parts of Chile; in Australia,

IS IT ALL IN THE SOIL?

Winemakers in different parts of the world disagree when it comes to the importance of soil in the production of good wine. The French believe that *terroir*—which means not just the soil, but also the elevation and aspect of the land—is the most important factor. American and Australian producers tend to feel that technology is paramount.

However, unhindered by the European idea of appellation or defined areas of origin, new world producers are freer to experiment and discover which soils are best for particular grape varieties.

STAG'S LEAP WINERY IN THE NAPA VALLEY

There are a number of fruit flavors associated with particular red grape varieties. Not all wines made from these grape varieties will exhibit the flavors listed, but many will.

Black currant: Cabernet Sauvignon, Cabernet Franc, Merlot, Syrah/Shiraz

Blackberry: Grenache/Garnacha, Zinfandel, young Syrah/Shiraz

Cherry: Beaujolais and other Gamay wines, young Barbera, Sangiovese

Plum: Young California Pinot Noir, Valpolicella, Syrah/Shiraz, Merlot, Grenache/Garnacha

Raspberry: Young French Pinot Noir, Gamay and Cabernet Franc, young Syrah/Shiraz

Strawberry: Young French Pinot Noir, Gamay, Tempranillo

In France, Cabernet Sauvignon forms a part of the blend in all the red wines of Bordeaux. It is the most important grape in the Médoc, where it is blended with smaller amounts of Merlot and Cabernet Franc. In St-Emilion it is much less important, taking third place in the blend after Cabernet Franc and Merlot.

Innovative winemakers such as Miguel Torres in the Penedès region of Spain also use Cabernet Sauvignon grapes in their blends. Examples are Coronas, Gran Coronas, and Gran Coronas Mas la Plana, which is colloquially known as "Black Label."

particularly in the Margaret River area; on New Zealand's South Island, and in Romania.

Now taste wine E. Think about how fruity it is and write a note on the aromas and flavors you find. How does it compare with wine D?

Cabernet Sauvignon is grown all over the world. It is made into single varietal wine in California, Oregon, Washington State, most parts of Australia, New Zealand, Chile, South Africa, Bulgaria, Hungary and the rest of central Europe, and the South of France. In some of these areas it is also blended with Merlot, Syrah/Shiraz or other grape varieties.

Cabernet Sauvignon is unusual in that it maintains a recognizable character and style wherever it is grown. The vines of Rutherford Bench in California's Napa Valley produce wines that rival, and indeed are sometimes mistaken for, those of the Médoc in France.

Have you written down black currant as part of your description? This is a common flavor comparison for wines made from Cabernet Sauvignon. But it is not always present and even when it is it varies quite a lot. Sometimes the perception is of fresh raw fruit and sometimes of cooked fruit. At others it is black currant cordial or black currant jam. Here again, your own perceptions of the aromas and flavors are the ones to note.

These impressions can be indicative of the origins

of the wine. For example, thoroughly ripe grapes grown in warm climates can give a sweet jammy flavor to the wine. If the weather gets too hot, the wine can end up tasting hot or even burnt.

Other overtones in the flavor of the wine will give you clues to how the wine was made. Wines that were bottled without being matured in wood will have much fresher fruit flavors than those that were. The age of the wine will also affect the taste of the fruit. The older it is the less fruit it is likely to retain.

Now taste wine F. Think about how fruity it is and write a note on the aromas and flavors you find. How does it compare with D and E?

Crozes-Hermitage comes from the upper Rhône Valley in France and is made from the Syrah grape. This grape variety is also used to make the better quality and longer-lasting Hermitage, Cornas and Côte Rotie wines.

Chocolate, coffee, and tar are the words most commonly used to describe the serious wines made from the Syrah grape, but when young their taste is sometimes described as reminiscent of black currant candy.

Young Crozes-Hermitage is usually quite tannic, and this quality can mask the fruit extract. If yours is a young wine you must decide whether or not the fruit will eventually come out to balance the tannins. The clues will be on the nose and the finish, so try to disregard the tannic center.

In the southern Rhône, Syrah goes

MERLOT

In the Napa Valley, Merlot was traditionally blended with Cabernet Sauvignon and Cabernet Franc to make wines in the Bordeaux style. However, Merlot is now emerging as a varietal in its own right, particularly in California's Sonoma Valley and Carneros, and in Washington State.

into quite a few of the blended wines that are characteristic of this area. These wines used to be very variable. Today, a number of winemakers are using a method called carbonic maceration to increase the fruit extract in their wines and to reduce the tannin levels. This method is explained on page 53.

Taste wines D, E and F again. Check that the notes you have made on all three wines will help you to recognize varietal characteristics in similar wines in the future.

Look at the labels on the bottles and note the age and origin of each wine as well as any information there might be about the production and maturation methods used. This will help you to analyze the findings of your nose and palate.

Complete the tasting by checking through your mnemonic, making full notes on the color, nose and palate of each wine. On the nose use your mnemonic for CGFIWM. On the palate remember FSATBBF. Transfer your notes to the notebook.

WOOD FLAVORS

One of the major decisions a winemaker has to make is how to mature his wine. Will it be sufficient to leave the fermented wine in concrete or stainless steel tanks until it is bottled or should it be matured in wood? If so, in what kind of wood and for how long?

In the traditional wine-making regions of the world these decisions are determined by custom or by the local wine-making laws. In California and other newer wine-producing regions, winemakers are free to experiment and use whatever method will give them the kind of wine that they want.

Maturation in wood gives a wine more complicated flavors. As well as showing the fruit extract, sugar, acidity and tannin which are already present in the grape juice, the wine will also take up some aromas and flavors from the wood itself. Over time all these elements should blend together to produce a well-balanced and complex wine.

The type of wood used, the size and age of the barrels and the length of time that the wine remains in the barrel, all affect the taste of the mature wine. Oak is the predominant wood used to make barrels, and new oak can impart a particularly distinctive vanilla-like aroma to the wine.

Red wine is more likely to be matured in oak barrels than white wine, but there were always some notable exceptions to this rule. In recent years winemakers in America, Australia and Chile have started to use new oak barrels to age a variety of wines made from different white grape varieties.

Wine that has been treated in this way has become so popular that all kinds of wines that in the past would not have been oaked are now matured in oak barrels. In fact, some producers are using shortcuts to give their wine the characteristic aroma and flavor of oak, such as throwing oak chips into the vat with the wine.

WOOD IN RED WINE

Pour wines A, B, C and D. Begin by tasting wine A. Is it fresh and fruity or vegetal and mature in character? Make a note on the aromas and flavors you find.

Whichever wine you have chosen for A, it is likely to be very fresh and fruity. These wines are made to be drunk within a year or two of the vintage or harvest and do not usually spend any time in wooden barrels. Italian wine that are labeled "Superiore" or "Classico" may be more mature. Check the vintage on the bottle.

THE WINES

A. LIGHT RED WINE
*such as Bardolino or Valpolicella,
or a light blended wine from California or
from a French Vin de Pays region*

B. GOOD RED BORDEAUX

C. CROZES-HERMITAGE
from the Rhône, Barolo from Italy or
Dão from Portugal*

D. RIOJA CRIANZA OR
OAK-AGED AUSTRALIAN
CABERNET SAUVIGNON*

E. UN-OAKED CHARDONNAY*
*from one of the Vin de Pays regions
of France, from Italy or eastern Europe,
or an un-oaked white Rioja from Spain*

F. OAK-AGED CHARDONNAY
*from California or Australia,
or an oak-aged white Rioja*

---

* You may have some of these wines left from earlier tastings. Ask your wine merchant for typical examples of oaked and un-oaked wines.

Vin de Pays, or regional wines, were introduced in France in 1981. They are wines of a more distinctive character and of slightly better quality than anonymous table wines. There are named Vin de Pays areas in all the wine-growing regions of France. The wines are usually light and fruity and may be made from a blend of grapes or from a single variety.

When wine is matured or aged in wood it starts to take on new aromas and flavors that come from the wood itself. These aromas are many and varied. Some are simply described as light wood, others more definitely as cedarwood or vanilla. The experts reserve the word "woody" to describe wine that has spent too long in wood and has lost its fruit flavors and become dull and dusty. You are unlikely to find any of these flavors in wine A.

Now taste wine B. Do you think that this wine has been matured in wood? Make a note on the aromas and flavors you find.

The red wines of Bordeaux are traditionally matured in oak barrels known as *barriques*. The finest wines—Premiers Crus or First Growths—are all matured in new oak. Lesser wines use about one third new barrels, with the rest of the wine going into barrels used in previous vintages. The matured wines are blended before bottling. Some wines may not see any new oak at all.

In Bordeaux, wood is used to help soften the wine and though it does impart an extra dimension to the wine the wood flavors are not intended to be predominant. The wine stays in *barriques* for anything from a few months to a couple of years. It is then bottled and left to mature for a further length of time before being sold. This might be months or years, depending on the quality of the wine.

The better the wine the longer it will need to mature in bottle before it is ready to drink. In Bordeaux the time that the wine spends maturing in the bottle is more important than that spent in wood. Premiers Crus, for example, may spend up to twenty years in bottle before they are ready to drink. The

MAKING *BARRIQUES* AT CHATEAU MARGAUX

AMARONE AND RECIOTO DELLA VALPOLICELLA

There are two styles of Valpolicella that you might come across which are quite unlike the usual light and fruity wines of this appellation, but they are also made in the Veneto.

They are Amarone della Valpolicella and Recioto della Valpolicella. These wines are made from selected grapes that are semi-dried on mats laid out in the sun before being fermented in the normal way.

Amarone is rich in style but with a very dry finish. It can last for twenty years. Recioto is rich and sweet and it, too, improves with age.

classification levels of fine Bordeaux wines are explained on page 80.

How have you described your sample of Bordeaux? Have you used words such as "cedarwood," "tobacco" or "cigarette box"?

These are all words commonly used to describe the wood aromas in classic Bordeaux wines. If you have paid enough for it, your wine will probably have seen some new oak, but because the emphasis in this region is on bottle-aging rather than on wood-aging the wines made here do not exhibit the vanilla tones so characteristic of wines from Rioja where all the wines are matured for quite long spells in new oak.

🍷 Are these flavors and aromas dominant or are they in balance with the other components of the wine?

Remember that if you have chosen a wine that is only about two or three years old it may not yet have developed its full potential. Young wines can be somewhat harsh and unbalanced and may have very little nose at all.

Bordeaux is the largest wine-producing region of France and the range of wines it produces is huge. There are simple red Bordeaux wines on sale at very reasonable prices. Then there are the "petit châteaux" or wines from small estates which do not qualify for one of the higher appellations explained below. Finally there are the Premiers and Grands Crus wines of Graves, the Médoc and St-Emilion.

Oak barrels are expensive and so is the time the wine spends in them. The longer a producer hangs on to his wine the longer it is before he realizes his investment. So if you have chosen one of the cheaper wines it may not have seen enough wood to show the characteristic qualities of good Bordeaux but it may still be a very pleasant wine to drink.

Indeed, too much wood may very

well be worse than too little. There is a tendency to think that first-class Bordeaux is all wood and no fruit. This is certainly not the case. If you are lucky enough to taste one of the great wines of Bordeaux at its peak you will find that it is still bursting with rich fruity flavors that are in perfect harmony with the woods and tannins.

🍷 Now taste wine C. Make a note on the aromas and flavors you find. How does it compare with wines A and B?

Whichever of the wines listed under C you have chosen you can be sure that it will be totally unlike the other wines in this tasting. These are big tannic wines that need long maturation to soften and tame them. The Crozes-Hermitage from the northern Rhône is probably the most approachable of the three wines. It will be ready to drink at an earlier age and will not be quite so tannic at any stage.

The wine from this part of France is transferred, after fermentation, to large wooden hogsheads that hold thousands of liters. Then, depending on the vintage and the quality of the wine, it stays there for two, three or even four years.

If you have chosen your Crozes-Hermitage well, you will find an earthy, vegetal aroma, perhaps with some raspberry fruit coming through after a moment or two. Chocolate, coffee and tar are often used to describe the palate. There is no cedarwood or vanilla; instead the wood imparts a peppery, smoky taste to the wine.

If you have chosen a Barolo you can expect an even thicker, more chewy wine than the Crozes-

Five Premiers Crus or First Growth estates represent the pinnacle of French wine-making in Bordeaux. They are Château Lafite-Rothschild, Château Latour, Château Margaux, Château Mouton-Rothschild and Château Haut-Brion. Wines from these estates cost a great deal when they are first released and even more as they mature.

However, there are other wines from Bordeaux that are considered to be just as good as the Médoc and Graves Premier Crus. They include Château Cheval Blanc and Château Ausone, both St-Emilion Premier Cru Classé wines, and Château Pétrus in Pomerol.

comments can be made about Dão wines from Portugal. "Dusty," "sawdust," and even "cardboard" are all words that might occur to you to describe wines that have been aged for a long time in old barrels.

However, things are beginning to change in both the Barolo and Dão regions. Some winemakers are experimenting with small oak barrels and they are all concentrating on making wines that are easier to drink by preserving the ripe fruitiness and relying less on excessive aging.

Now taste wine D. Make a note on the aromas and flavors you find. How does it compare with wines A, B, and C?

Hermitage. Italy is the land of large wooden barrels. There is no tradition here, as there is in Bordeaux and Burgundy, of laying down bottles for the future. Most wine is matured in wood.

Barolo wines are often so tough that they need a long time to soften, perhaps as much as six to eight years. The problem is that this could add to the tannin levels and be too long for the fruit to survive, leaving the wine dull and dried out. Take care, though, before you pronounce your sample woody. It may just be too young! Top quality Barolo wine really does benefit from all that time in wood, becoming superbly complex and interesting.

The same sort of

Whether you have chosen a wine from the classic Spanish region of Rioja or an oak-aged wine from California or Australia, the chances are that you will now pick up a definite whiff of vanilla.

Most Rioja spends a good deal of time maturing in new oak barrels or *barricas*. The better the wine, the longer it stays in *barricas,* and the quality ratings for Rioja are based on this element of its production.

Rioja can be made from seven different grape varieties, but the predominant variety is Tempranillo. You may also come across this variety under the name of Cencibel in wines from La Mancha. Expect to find plenty of ripe fruit along with the vanilla on the nose of good Rioja and, depending on its age, a vegetal maturity.

The quality ratings for red Rioja are Sin Crianza which literally means without oak, but even these wines may nevertheless have spent a few months in cask. Con Crianza wine must be matured for two years with a minimum of one in barrel. Reserva wines must be matured for three years with a minimum of one year in barrel. Gran Reserva wine must be matured for at least three years in barrel and two in bottle, or vice versa.

A few years ago you could be sure that all Aus-tralian Cabernet Sauvignon wines would have a good slug of oak in them. Indeed, it could often be argued that there was too much. Today Australian winemakers have become much more sophisticated and producers are making wines to their own styles. Some wines have remained very oaky, but others are showing more of their fresh fruit flavors.

In the Coonawarra region of South Australia, producers are blending Cabernet Sauvignon with a little Merlot and Cabernet Franc. The style they are achieving is surprisingly close to that of Bordeaux. The wines have a cedar and truffle-like aroma with plenty of fruit on the palate.

CLEANING A BARREL

Taste wines A, B, C and D again then check the notes you have made on all four wines. Do you think that these notes will help you to remember the basic differences between the wines or do you need to add a little more?

Look at the labels on the bottles and note the age and origin of each wine and any information there might be about the produc-tion and maturation methods used. This will help you to analyze the findings of your nose and palate.

WOOD IN WHITE WINE

Most white wines are much more delicate than red wines and as a result do not stand up as easily to the assault of aging in new oak barrels. However, there have always been some notable exceptions in classic areas and these have been augmented in recent years by many of the wines from the newer wine-making regions of the world.

🍷 Pour wines E and F. Taste wine E and make a note on the aromas and flavors you find.

Whatever wine you have chosen for E, it is likely to be fresh and fruity. The actual depth of fruit and its flavor will depend upon where it comes from, but there will be no wood to complicate the aromas.

🍷 Now taste wine F. Make a note on the aromas and flavors you find and compare it to wine E.

If you have chosen a California Chardonnay from one of the wineries listed below, or an Australian Chardonnay, particularly one from Coonawarra, you can expect it to be full of lush, ripe almost oily fruit. Because it has been matured in oak, you can also expect to find that distinctive vanilla aroma.

🍷 Do you think that the description "buttery" can be applied to either of the wines?

MATURING WHITE WINES IN NEW OAK

Words or phrases such as oak-aged, oaked, oak influenced, barrel matured, *barrique*-aged or *cuvée bois* on a label suggest that the wine it contains may have been kept in new oak barrels. However, if the words barrel or cask are not included in the description you might suspect that oak chips have been added to the wine in the vat.

The producers listed here often use a good deal of oak, though not necessarily in all their wines. Check with your wine store before buying.

CALIFORNIA:	AUSTRALIA:	CHILE:	BURGUNDY:	SPAIN:
Au Bon Climat	Angove's Reserve wines	Concha y Toro	Domaine Dujac	Agramont
Dunn	Berri Estates/Renmano	Cousino Macul	Dauvissat (Chablis)	Ardanza
Grace Family Vineyard	McGuigan	Los Vascos	Faiveley	Cune (white)
Groth	Tyrells	Santa Carolina	Lafon	Lopez de Heredia
Pine Ridge	Wyndham Estates	Valdivieso	Olivier Laflaive Frères	Marqués de Murrieta
Sanford (Chardonnay)	Wynns's Coonawarra wines		Tollot-Beaut et Fils	Navajas (white)

You may have heard the word buttery used in conjunction with Chardonnay wines. The oiliness of some Chardonnay may indeed suggest butter, but you may not find this characteristic on European Chardonnays. A number of professionals maintain that the buttery aroma of some Chardonnay wines comes not from their fruit extract, but from the new oak barrels in which they are matured. Others believe that it is the combination of new oak and the malolactic fermentation (see page 117) that contribute to this characteristic.

🍷 **Taste wine F again and make a note on the degree of oak in the wine. Do you think it is excessive or light? Is it in balance with the other components of the wine?**

The strength of the oaky vanilla flavors in the wine will depend upon the length of time that the wine has spent in new oak. Some wines have sufficient fruit extract to survive for quite a long time, others are swamped after only a few months. An over-oaked and unbalanced wine can be an indication that the producer has used oak chips to flavor the wine instead of maturing it in new oak barrels.

In deciding whether or not you think a wine has spent too long in oak you must bear in mind your own personal taste. A wine may well be in balance but have too much oak for you. Other people may love this particular style.

Whatever their strength, the oaky flavors in California and Australian Chardonnays have become very popular. As a result producers all over the wine-making world, including Europe, South Africa and Chile, are starting to oak-age wines made from other grape varieties. Sometimes the results are startlingly good, sometimes not.

It has become increasingly difficult to find a white Rioja that has been matured in oak. A few years ago many of the winemakers of Rioja decided to do away with oak-aging in white wine. They now produce squeaky-clean wines that are hard to distinguish from other cold-fermentation wines made elsewhere in Europe. Today there are only a handful of bodegas or wineries maturing their white wine in barrels or *barricas*. They include Marqués de Murrieta and Cune.

🍷 **Complete the tasting by checking through your mnemonic, making full notes on the color, nose and palate of each wine. On the nose use your mnemonic for CGFIWM. On the palate remember FSATBBF. Transfer your notes to the notebook.**

NEW OAK IN THE US

The amount of new oak that comes through on the nose of American Cabernet Sauvignon wines varies considerably. Robert Mondavi, for example, often strives for a Bordeaux style and his wines do not show a lot of new oak vanilla. If you would like to include an oak-aged Cabernet Sauvignon wine from California in the tasting check the label for words such as "Private Reserve" or "Proprietor's Selection." This usually means that the wine is made from a particularly good selection of grapes and it is likely to have seen more new wood aging than other wines.

NICE AND EASY OR ROBUST?

Y ou have probably found that some wines seem very light and easy to drink, whereas others require much more effort to appreciate their qualities. This difference in the feeling in the mouth or in the texture of the wine is known as "mouthfeel" or body. Wines can be light, medium, or full-bodied depending on the different qualities present.

Fruit extract, tannin and alcohol all contribute to the body of a wine. The higher the level of any of these three components, the fuller the wine will seem. If all three are present together in some quantity you will have a very heavy or full-bodied wine. The presence of sugar also deepens the texture of wine, giving it more body.

All these components vary according to the excellence or otherwise of the vintage, the geographical origin of the wine and the way in which it is made and matured. Thus, wines made in years when the weather conditions are just right for a good vintage are inclined to have more body than those made when the weather is poor. Wines made in hotter climates, too, tend to have more body than those from cooler ones. In the northern hemisphere this means southern regions such as Rioja and Tuscany, and in the southern hemisphere the Hunter Valley in Australia and the northern part of Chile.

Some wine-making decisions are dictated by the local wine laws, others are made by the producer, but however they are made decisions to use a different method of fermentation or to age in oak barrels will make the wine lighter or heavier.

Some wines have brandy added to them before the fermentation process is complete. This results in what is known as fortified wine in Europe and dessert wine in America. These wines are much higher in alcohol than table wines. They are often very sweet, have plenty of fruit extract and are extremely full-bodied.

BODY IN RED WINE

Pour wines A, B and C. Taste wine A then wine B thinking specifically about the mouthfeel or body. Which is the heavier wine?

The Gamay grape gives Beaujolais a juicy, fruity flavor without very much complexity. The Cabernet Sauvignon, too, will have plenty of fruit but it will also have more depth and complexity. Whatever Beaujolais or Cabernet you have chosen you can be sure of finding a good deal of difference between the two.

Most Beaujolais is made to be drunk within a year; some, such as Beaujolais Nouveau, is sold within a few weeks of being harvested. Other Beaujolais

---

THE WINES

A. BEAUJOLAIS

B. CABERNET SAUVIGNON★
from California★, Chile★ or Australia

C. GOOD RUBY PORT

D. NIERSTEINER KABINETT
from Germany★

E. CHARDONNAY
*from California★, Chile★ or
New Zealand★*

F. FINO SHERRY
OR
MEDIUM DRY SHERRY
SUCH AS AMONTILLADO

★*You may have some of these
wines left from earlier tastings.*

---

wines, however, are made to last a little longer and will be a bit fuller than the basic Beaujolais.

Beaujolais Villages, for example, or a Beaujolais from one of ten specifically named "crus" or villages, do have more body, but they still do not usually reach the levels of Cabernet Sauvignon wines. Popular Beaujolais crus are Fleurie, Morgon, Julienas and Moulin-à-Vent.

Depending on which wine you have chosen, the Cabernet Sauvignon may have been made to be drunk within a couple of years or it may have been designed to last rather longer. Cheaper wines and mass-produced brands will be lighter than wines that command a higher price.

They are cheaper because they have not been made using the best grapes from the best areas and they have not spent a lot of costly time in wood. The factors that make for an economical wine are the opposite of those that make for a full-bodied wine.

Wines from top estates, such as Robert Mondavi's Opus One from California, Château Latour from Bordeaux or Le Corton from Burgundy, are rich and full-bodied. They have had the best of everything!

Which of these two wines do you like best? Do you think that you would like wines which are heavier than these two?

CARBONIC MACERATION

A special process has been developed in the Beaujolais region to make the most of the juicy cherry flavors of the Gamay grape. The grapes are not pressed. Instead, the uncrushed grapes are piled into vats and covered.

As fermentation starts at the base of the vat the carbon dioxide, which is given off in the normal way, rises up the vat and envelops the uncrushed grapes above. These then start to ferment inside their skins. This process is also used in the southern part of the Rhône Valley in France to produce wines that are much more approachable and easy to drink than some of the traditional wines. It is also gaining ground in the Languedoc-Roussillon. (The label will not tell you if the wine was made this way, so ask your wine merchant.)

The process ensures the maximum extraction of color and flavor, leaving the tannins behind in the skins. Wines that have been produced using the carbonic maceration process have a characteristic slightly "cabbagey" aroma.

Some wine-producing areas are famous for making very heavy wines. Cahors, in southwest France, is famous for its "black wine." Made from the Malbec grape, this wine is extremely tannic. There are still producers in Cahors who make this kind of wine, but others now prefer to make a lighter, fruitier wine. Unfortunately, is often difficult to tell from the label which is which.

Australian winemakers make their own very tannic, full-bodied wines from the Shiraz grape variety. (Shiraz is the Australian name for the Syrah grape, but the term is also used in South Africa and elsewhere in the new world.) By no means all wines made from Shiraz are like this, but a famous example is Penfolds Grange Hermitage, the Château Latour of the southern hemisphere.

In California, Zinfandel can also produce really full-bodied wines that are the focus of the "Zin" fan club. However, this is such a versatile grape variety that it is also used to make light fruity red wines and even off-white or blush wines. The latter are discussed on page 90.

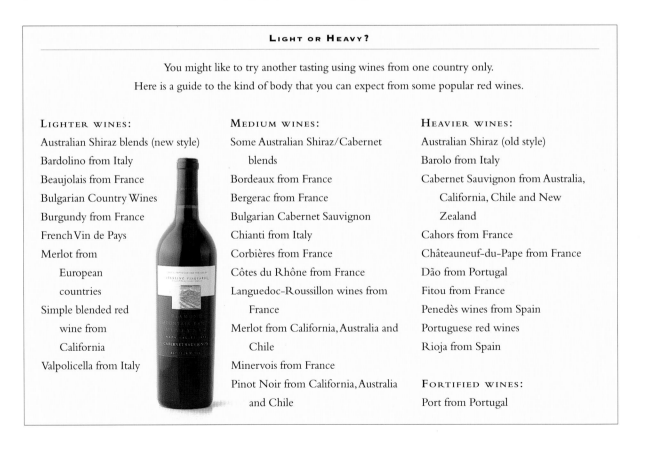

LIGHT OR HEAVY?

You might like to try another tasting using wines from one country only.
Here is a guide to the kind of body that you can expect from some popular red wines.

LIGHTER WINES:
Australian Shiraz blends (new style)
Bardolino from Italy
Beaujolais from France
Bulgarian Country Wines
Burgundy from France
French Vin de Pays
Merlot from
    European
    countries
Simple blended red
    wine from
    California
Valpolicella from Italy

MEDIUM WINES:
Some Australian Shiraz/Cabernet
    blends
Bordeaux from France
Bergerac from France
Bulgarian Cabernet Sauvignon
Chianti from Italy
Corbières from France
Côtes du Rhône from France
Languedoc-Roussillon wines from
    France
Merlot from California, Australia and
    Chile
Minervois from France
Pinot Noir from California, Australia
    and Chile

HEAVIER WINES:
Australian Shiraz (old style)
Barolo from Italy
Cabernet Sauvignon from Australia,
    California, Chile and New
    Zealand
Cahors from France
Châteauneuf-du-Pape from France
Dão from Portugal
Fitou from France
Penedès wines from Spain
Portuguese red wines
Rioja from Spain

FORTIFIED WINES:
Port from Portugal

THE BAROSSA VALLEY, SOUTH AUSTRALIA

FRUIT AND TANNIN IN RED WINE

Taste wines A and B again. This time think specifically about the depth of fruit extract in the wines and their tannin levels.

Both wines probably have plenty of fruit, but the Cabernet Sauvignon is likely to have fuller, deeper fruit flavors because this grape variety naturally produces wines with more fruit extract.

Your wine may appear to have a lot of fruit if it comes from an area where the climate is very warm and the grapes have ripened well. McLaren Vale and the Barossa Valley in Australia, for example, both produce very full-bodied wines.

Tannin can be detected by the harsh "furry" feel it leaves on your tongue and on the back of your teeth. Some experts describe wine with high fruit extract and high tannin levels as "chewy." Very tannic wines can be softened by food.

Taste wine A again. Do you think that the tannin is in balance with the fruit extract and acidity? Repeat the process with wine B.

If all of the elements are in balance then the wine is probably ready to drink. If it is not in balance, the wine may simply be too young to drink. Young wines that have been designed to last will have a good deal of tannin in them. This tannin should soften over time and come into balance with the other components of the wine. On the other hand, it may be that the wine is just not very good!

The points to bear in mind when making this kind of assessment are: the price of the wine; the standing of the appellation; the reputation of the producer, and the aromas and finish of the wine. However, this is not an exact science and not even the experts get it right every time.

ALCOHOL AND LABELS

The percentage alcohol by volume in a wine is usually stated on the label. Another sign of higher alcohol in French wines is the appearance of the word "Supérieur" on the bottle. This usually indicates that the wine has a higher degree of alcohol than the basic wine. For example, there is a minimum alcoholic degree of 10.5 percent for Bordeaux Supérieur against 10 percent for Bordeaux.

In the United States there are no hard and fast rules, but a wine labeled "Private Reserve," or "Special Selection" or or words to that effect, is likely to be high in alcohol.

ALCOHOL LEVELS IN RED WINE

Taste wines A and B again then wine C. Do you think that the ascending level of alcohol is obvious to the taste?

Alcohol itself does not really have any taste, but wines with high alcohol levels feel very much fuller in the mouth.

The alcoholic content of wine is expressed as a percentage of the volume. Table wines come in at around 8 to 15 percent alcohol by volume. This may not seem like a very wide range, but it is surprising the difference that even half a percent can make to the mouthfeel of a wine.

Ordinary table wine is unlikely to reach a high level of alcohol, as fermentation will not continue once 15 percent alcohol by volume is reached. The yeasts cannot tolerate this level of alcohol and die.

Wine from the top estates, wherever they are, also tend to be higher in alcohol (as well as in fruit extract and tannin) because every effort is made to ensure that the grapes reach their optimum sugar levels.

Fortified wine and American dessert wines have alcohol added to them either during or after fermentation. They range from around 15 percent to 22 percent by volume.

In contrast, the alcohol content of Beaujolais is not usually all that high. Burgundy—where Beaujolais is made—is quite far north in wine-growing terms and typical examples contain about 11 to 12 percent alcohol by volume. Check the label on your bottle to see exactly what level of alcohol the wine contains.

Cabernet Sauvignon wines vary in their alcohol

STYLES OF PORT

All port is made by fermenting sweet red grapes. The fermentation is stopped at quite an early stage by the addition of grape brandy. Because the fermentation is not complete the wine retains much of its fruity flavors and has a high degree of residual sugar.

There are many styles of port and these can be confusing to the uninitiated. Here is a round up of the styles most easily found outside Portugal.

Ruby: This is aged in oak casks for about three to four years before blending and bottling. It has a bright ruby color and a simple, fruity flavor. Some producers give their best ruby ports name like Special Reserve, Vintage Style or Chairman's Reserve.

Aged Tawny: This is kept in cask for longer than ruby port. The best will have an age (an average of the age of the blends) of some ten to twenty years. It has a tawny color and a full nutty and dried fruit flavor.

Vintage: This is made only from the very finest grapes in a great year. A vintage year is declared when the producer is sure he will have the best material with which to work. Vintage port starts off in the same way as ruby port but is bottled much earlier, usually after twenty-two to thirty-one months. It then matures in the bottle for five to twenty-five years. It has a deep brick red color and a complex fruity flavor. This wine produces a sediment that accumulates in the bottle in the years that it is maturing so vintage port is one of the few wines which need to be decanted.

Late Bottled Vintage: This wine is made from the grapes of a single harvest but it is matured in barrel for longer than vintage port and so produces all its sediment in the cask rather than in the bottle. It has a deep red color and a full and fruity flavor.

Most port producers also make a white port. This wine is made in just the same way as port but with white rather than red grapes. It may be sweet or dry and is best drunk chilled as an aperitif.

content. Varietal Vin de Pays wines such Vin de Pays d'Oc or Vin de Pays de l'Hérault from the South of France may be as low as 11 to 12 percent by volume. Cabernet Sauvignon wines from California are likely to be higher at around 12 to 13.5 percent.

Most Australian varietal wines reach much the same levels, but some Cabernet Sauvignon wines can reach 14 or even 14.5 percent. If you have chosen a wine from Chile, you should also expect it to be fairly high in alcohol. Check the label for the exact level of your wine.

The port (wine C) will taste very much fuller and heavier than either of the first two wines. This is because its elevated alcohol content combines with a high degree of fruit and sugar to give a great deal more body. You will probably have picked up the extra alcohol on the nose of this wine.

Think about the finish of each wine. Do you detect any bitter or burning sensations?

Wines that are high in alcohol sometimes have a bitter aftertaste or finish. You may even find that the tip of your tongue tingles when tasting these wines. Some professionals describe the sensation as a burning sensation.

STYLES OF SHERRY

Unlike port, sherry starts out as a fully fermented dry white wine. It is eventually fortified with grape brandy to 15 to 22 percent by volume. In Spain almost all the wines remain dry but, with the exception of manzanilla and fino sherry, they are sweetened for export.

After the wine has been fortified it is put into a cask with a gap between the level of the wine and the top of the barrel. In some barrels a layer of "flor" or yeast grows on the top of the wine, keeping out the air. In others it does not. Each wine is used to make a different sherry.

There are no vintages in sherry. All sherries are blends of many years and the blending is done by a special system known as the "solera" system. A certain percentage of the wine is drawn off the barrels at one end of the system and bottled. These barrels are topped up with sherry from the next barrels down the line and so on until the youngest barrels are topped up with the new vintage.

The different styles of sherry are:

Manzanilla: This is a flor-based sherry that is matured exclusively on the coast at Sanlúcar de Barrameda. The wine is dry and delicate, and some would say salty.

Fino: This, too, is a flor-based sherry that is produced anywhere in the Jerez region. It is dry and distinctive.

Amontillado: This wine is made from flor-based wines that are not considered good enough to bottle. They are left in the cask until the flor dies away and the wine takes on a nutty flavor. Amontillado may be dry or sweet.

Oloroso: This wine develops without any flor and so becomes oxidized. It has a strong and distinctive flavor that develops over time. It too may be sweet or dry.

NICE AND EASY OR ROBUST?

BODY IN WHITE WINE

Pour wines D, E and F. Taste wine D then wine E. Make a note on the aromas, flavors and mouthfeel of the wines. Which do you think is the heavier wine?

There is less variation in the body of white wines than red wines and most dry white wines can be described as light or medium bodied. Heavier wines include old-style oaked Rioja, and oaked wines from the hotter parts of Australia and Chile.

The wine-producing areas of Germany are situated at the climatic limits for the cultivation of grapes. In some years there simply is not enough sunshine to ripen the grapes to their full extent. As a result some German wines can be a little thin and acidic.

To overcome this problem, everyday wines may have sugar added to them in the form of "Süsswein" or unfermented grape juice. This goes in just before the wine is bottled. The practice is not allowed for German quality wines which must have sufficient sugar to reach the set standards. See page 28 for more information on these wines.

In contrast, Chardonnay from California, Chile or New Zealand is likely to have more body. These wine-producing areas have a more extreme climate than Germany and you can expect plenty of fruit extract and quite intense flavors. Natural sugar levels will be higher. This does not mean that the wines will be sweet as the sugar is fermented out to give a higher alcohol content.

CHILEAN VINEYARD IN THE UPPER MAIPO VALLEY

Because, unlike red wine, white wines are not fermented on their skins there is no tannin to consider, but the residual sugar levels can affect the mouthfeel, giving a velvety texture to the wine. For example, most German white wines are medium dry or medium sweet and this can affect your assessment of their body. The Niersteiner has plenty of fruity flavors and a touch of velvet, but once swallowed is not at all memorable.

🔩 **Turn back to the notes you made on the sweet white wines sampled in Tasting 2: the Moscatel de Valencia (wine E) and the Sauternes (wines F).**

Both wines had a very velvety mouthfeel. They also had a very definite depth of flavor that lingered in the mouth. The Sauternes could definitely be described as a full-bodied white wine.

ALCOHOL IN WHITE WINE

🔩 **Taste wines D and E again then wine F. Do you think that the ascending levels of alcohol are obvious to the taste?**

The alcoholic content of everyday German wine is rarely much higher than 11 percent by volume and could be quite a lot less. Check the label on your bottle to see exactly what level of alcohol it contains.

Compare this with the level given on the Chardonnay label. If you have chosen a Chilean Chardonnay the chances are that the alcohol content could be as high as 13 or 13.5 percent by volume. Californian and New Zealand wines vary a good deal, but they usually contain around 11.5 to13 percent alcohol by volume.

The sherry will certainly taste fuller and heavier than either of the first two wines. This will be the case even if you have chosen a bone dry fino sherry. The reason is, of course, the elevated alcohol content. If you have chosen a medium dry Amontillado the rich nutty flavors will add to the impression of body.

🔩 **Think about the finish of each wine. Do you detect any bitter or burning sensations?**

Do not be surprised if you do not particularly notice the alcohol level of the Chardonnay wine. In the warmer parts of the world, wine made from this grape variety is usually rich enough to balance the alcohol. The lush fruit masks any bitterness the alcohol may impart.

This is not always the case with wine made from other grape varieties. If Sauvignon Blanc reaches the 13 to 13.5 percent level, as often happens with Sauvignon Blanc from Chile, the result can be very bitter indeed.

🔩 **Complete the tasting by checking through your mnemonic, making full notes on the color, nose and palate of each wine. On the nose use your mnemonic for CGFIWM. On the palate remember FSATBBF. Transfer your notes to the notebook.**

ASSESSING YOUR PROGRESS

In the previous tastings you have discovered what is meant by sweetness and dryness, acidity, fruit extract, wood, tannin, alcohol, body and balance in wine. You have tasted a range of wines showing all these attributes in varying degrees. An understanding of the basic taste components is the tool that you need to begin to assess wine in more depth and with more certainty than simply deciding whether or not you like it, important though this is.

Practice is very important in learning to taste wine effectively. Now that you are making a conscious effort to taste wine in an organized way you may be surprised by your progress. This tasting gives you the opportunity to assess how well you are doing and to review what was covered earlier.

Because a glance at the label will often disclose a great deal of information about a wine, it is suggested that you sample the wines in this tasting "blind." This refers to concealing the bottle—the shape of which can be a useful clue to its contents—as well as the label.

It is particularly important in this tasting to discuss your findings with the other tasters, as there are no "correct" answers that can be given in the text.

At a professional blind tasting the bottles are disguised in special padded bags, but this may not be feasible at home. One solution is to decant the wines into identical containers with hidden labels and shuffle them. Alternatively, take turns with your fellow tasters pouring the wine into glasses and bringing them in as required. Label the foot of each taster's glasses 1 to 7 so that the person pouring out the wines can keep track of which is which.

Conceal the list of wines shown at the beginning of this tasting and keep the bottles out of sight so that no one taking part knows which wines are included.

— THE WINES —

A. YOUR FAVORITE WHITE WINE

B. YOUR FAVORITE RED WINE

C. CHARDONNAY
from California★, Oregon, Washington State, Chile★, Burgundy (Chablis, Meursault or Montrachet), New Zealand★ or Australia★

D. GOOD QUALITY GERMAN RIESLING
at the Kabinett level

E. MOSCATEL DE VALENCIA
from Spain★ or Orange Muscat★ from California

F. LIGHT GAMAY OR GRENACHE/GARNACHA
from France, Spain or California

G. CABERNET SAUVIGNON
from California★, Washington State, Bulgaria or Chile★

★You may have some of these wines left from earlier tastings.

RECOGNIZING YOUR FAVORITES

If you would like to extend this tasting ask your friends to bring their favorite wines to add to this and the triangular tasting below.

Taste wines A, C and D and make a note on their color, aroma and flavors. On the nose use your mnemonic for CGFIWM. On the palate remember FSATBBF. Which wine do you think is your favorite and why?

You will probably recognize your favorite wine simply because you are so familiar with it. However, if your favorite wine is similar to wines C and D, it might be quite difficult to spot! Write a full note and when you have finished, look at what you have written to see if your notes point you in the right direction.

For example, if your chosen white wine comes from an area with a cool climate such as Muscadet in France or the Alto Adige Trentino in Italy you may have used words like "pale straw" or "light yellow" to describe the color; "light," "elegant," and "apple fresh" to describe the nose; and "apples," "pears," "touch of honey" and "short crisp finish" to describe the palate.

None of these descriptive words is exclusive to

wine from a particular region but, taken together, they could well point to one of the cooler wine producing regions such as Muscadet or the Alto Adige Trentino.

Where do you think the other wines might come from? Try to be as specific as you can and give your reasons.

You can, of course, have a look at the bottles now to see how you have fared but you will probably gain more from this tasting if you wait until you have finished all the exercises.

TRIANGULAR TASTING TO PICK THE ODD WINE OUT

This is a good test of the accuracy of your tasting. Each person needs two samples of one wine and one sample of another wine. The object of the exercise is to pick the odd one out. You can make it as easy or as difficult as you like simply by changing the choice of wines. For example, if your chosen wine (wine A) is another Chardonnay, taste it against wine C.

Wines C and D have been chosen because they should be reasonably easy to distinguish. They are made from specific grape varieties that have very

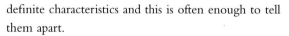

RIESLING VINEYARD ABOVE PIESPORT, GERMANY

definite characteristics and this is often enough to tell them apart.

If you decide to use your favorite wine and it has a very distinctive color that would easily give it away, you might like to use colored glasses or plastic cups for this one tasting.

Try the same tasting with red wines F and G, substituting your favorite (wine B) if you wish.

CHECKING THE TASTE COMPONENTS IN WHITE WINE

This blind tasting is designed to review your ability to recognize and evaluate the various taste components of wine covered in the previous tastings. These include sweetness and dryness, acidity, fruit extract, wood, tannin, alcohol, body and balance.

Because the tasting is blind you will not have any preconceived ideas or expectations of how the wines should taste and so you will be able to make an unbiased assessment.

Pour wines C, D and E. As you taste them concentrate particularly on the levels of fruit extract, sugar and acidity. Make a note on each of these components.

Try to assess each taste component separately.

What words have you used to describe the fruit in these wines? Can you identify the grape varieties from your descriptions or from your taste memory?

At the end of the session you can check the actual grape varieties on the labels.

ORANGE MUSCAT

Orange Muscat is the Californian name for the Italian Moscato Fior d'Arancio grape. It is used in wines like Andrew Quady's Essensia from Central Valley.

IDENTIFYING WHITE GRAPE VARIETIES

Chardonnay: Butter, honey, apple, pineapple, mango, tropical fruits

Gewürztraminer: Lychee, spice, pepper, flowers, roses

Muscadet: Apple, honey, stone

Muscat: Grape, orange rind

Riesling: Citrus fruit, grapefruit, flowers, oil, gasoline

Sauvignon Blanc: Gooseberry, fresh leaves, mint, grass, asparagus

Sémillon: Lemon, melon, pineapple, tropical fruits, peach, nuts, oil, lanolin

Trebbiano/Ugni Blanc: Almond, honey, minerals

Now concentrate on the sugar levels and place the wines in ascending order of sweetness.

One of the wines is very much sweeter than the others, but you may have some trouble assessing the remaining two. To some extent it will depend on the wines you have chosen, but the likely ranking is C, D, E. It is possible that you might have had some difficulty in deciding on the sweetness/dryness levels of wines C and D.

Keep the wines in your chosen order of sweetness. Now think about the acidity levels in the three wines. Do you think that their acidity might have affected your judgment of the sugar levels?

Remember that acidity is sometimes reminiscent of tart cooking apples and at others of lemon or grapefruit juice. Think about the way this component of the wine affected your perception of the wines in Tasting 2.

🍾 Is one of the wines **obviously more acidic than the others? Do you think that the wines are well balanced in terms of sugar and acidity?**

Discuss the wines with the other tasters and see if you can come to a consensus.

🍾 Taste the wines again and **think about wood, alcohol, body and balance Make notes on these too.**

On the basis of your full notes you may feel ready to guess from which wine-producing regions the wines come. Remember to consider the color and appearance of each wine as well as its nose and palate. Do you recognize a grape variety? Was the wine aged in oak? Remember, too, that the finish can tell you quite a lot about the wine.

If for wine C you chose a Chardonnay from one of the warmer wine-producing regions, such as California, Australia or Chile, you might have found that the acidity level of the wine was not very high. Add to this the very full flavor of ripe grapes from these regions and you may have thought that the wine was sweeter than it really was.

The German Riesling (wine D), on the other hand, would almost certainly have been medium dry at 3 to 5 on the European sweetness scale, but it might have tasted almost dry if it had good acidity. Wines like this are often described as "off-dry."

The Moscatel or Muscat should not have been too difficult to place as the sweetest wine in this tasting, but was it well balanced, cloying or over-acidic? Now look at the bottles. How well did you do?

FROG'S LEAP WINERY

CHECKING THE TASTE COMPONENTS IN RED WINE

Pour wines F and G. As you taste them concentrate particularly on the levels of fruit extract and tannin.

Both these wines have very definite aromas and flavors. Try to assess each taste component separately and make a note of what you find.

What words have you used to describe the fruit in these wines? Can you identify the grape varieties from your descriptions or from your taste memory?

At the end of the session you can check the actual grape varieties on the labels.

Taste wines F and G again. Which do you think is the most tannic?

One of the wines will have little or no tannin. Which do you think it is? Remember that tannin gives a "furry" feeling to the back of the teeth and the gums.

You should find that wine F has little or no tannin. Do you think that your favorite wine it is more or less tannic than wines F and G?

Taste the wines again and think about the other components, which include wood, alcohol, body and balance, and make notes on these too.

Before looking at the bottles try to assess from which regions the wines come. The clues will include the type of fruit flavors—you may have already decided upon a grape variety, the depth of intensity and the type of wood used. Remember, too, that the finish can tell you quite a lot about the wine. Do not forget to consider the color and appearance of the wine as well as the nose and palate.

IDENTIFYING RED GRAPE VARIETIES

Cabernet Franc: Black currant, grass, fresh leaves

Cabernet Sauvignon: Black currant, cedar, mint

Gamay: Cherry, raspberry, strawberry

Grenache/Garnacha: Blackberry, plum

Merlot: Black currant, plum, mint, raisins

Nebbiolo: Prune, raisins, tobacco and tar

Pinot Noir: Strawberries, plums, cooked beet, chocolate, farmyards, cheese, licorice

Sangiovese: Cherry, herbs, tobacco

Syrah/Shiraz: Raspberry, plum, black currant, chocolate, coffee, leather, tar, pepper

Zinfandel: Blackberry, berry fruits

WHAT'S IN A YEAR?

Wine is a dynamic product with a natural lifespan. It changes over time and whether this change is for the better or not is determined firstly by the age of the wine. A young wine is likely to benefit more from these changes than an older wine. The quality of the grapes used and the way in which they are turned into wine are also important.

However wine is stored after fermentation it slowly matures and undergoes a number of chemical changes. It also, very gradually, takes up oxygen. In the early stages these processes are beneficial to the wine and are deliberately used to improve it. They help to soften acidity and tannin levels, and contribute to the process necessary to create a fine wine. The better the wine the more it will stand up to, or even need, this evolution.

Winemakers are, above all, dependent on the quality of their raw materials—the grapes themselves. The weather conditions during the year affect the degree of ripeness the grapes achieve and thus the sugar, acidity and fruit extract levels of the wine made from them. A vintage chart records the growing conditions in the classic areas. "Vintage" simply means the year in which the grapes were ripened and harvested. Thus there is a vintage every year and this is the date carried on most bottles.

Many inexpensive wines that are made to be drunk within a year or two of the harvest do not appear on vintage charts because their long term potential is not very important.

On the other hand, if you are planning to buy wine and store it for future use you will want to know how it is likely to fare. By the same token, if you are buying fine wine from a merchant or in a restaurant you want to be sure that you are getting good value for your money. The date on the label coupled with a knowledge of the vintage can help a great deal.

Some wines, such as port and Champagne, *are* blends of wines from different years and so do not carry a specific date. However, in some years a vintage is "declared" by the producer, and these vintage ports and Champagnes are the product of one year only.

Winemakers declare a vintage only when the climatic conditions have been at their most favorable and the very best quality grapes have been produced.

Wines at the bottom end of the quality scale, such as basic Vins de Table and mass-produced wines, are also blends of different years and so

---

THE WINES

A, B AND C

USA:
CALIFORNIA CARNEROS
1994, 1990 or 1991, 1987

France:
POMEROL
1990, 1986 or 1985, 1982

NUITS ST-GEORGES
1990, 1988, 1985

MEDOC
1990, 1986 or 1985, 1982

Italy:
CHIANTI CLASSICO RESERVA
1994, 1990, 1988 or 1985

Spain:
RIOJA RESERVA
1994, 1990, 1987

D, E AND F

USA:
CALIFORNIA CARNEROS
1994, 1991, 1988

France:
SAUTERNES
1990, 1986, 1983

MEURSAULT
1992, 1990 or 1989, 1986

COTEAUX DU LAYON
1990, 1986 or 1985, 1983

Germany:
RHEINGAU
1992, 1989, 1985

---

do not carry a vintage date.

This tasting concentrates on the effect that the climatic conditions in one year have on the grapes— hence on the wine. It also looks at how wine matures and ages over time. For A, B and C select three wines from the same region and preferably from the same producer. For D, E and F choose three wines from one of those regions that specialize in white wines with ageing potential, preferably from the same producer. The wines suggested for this tasting are from some of the great wine-growing areas of the world, and the vintages given are among the best of the last two decades. Follow the Eight Steps to Tasting Wine set out at the beginning of Tasting 1.

AGING IN WINE

Many people think that the older a wine, the better it will be. In fact, a wine that would have been very good at five or ten years old may be ruined if kept for fifteen or twenty years. Even wines at the very top levels, such as Bordeaux Premiers Crus, Burgundy Grand Crus and the very best wines of California and Australia, which are designed to age for a long time, will eventually pass their prime. They just take rather longer than other wines to do so.

 Pour a glass of wine A, the youngest of your red wines. Make a note on the color, aroma and palate. Do you think that the wine is ready to drink?

The chances are that you will find the wine far too young to drink. It could be going through a closed phase and have little or no aroma. The acidity and tannins will be quite harsh and may well be masking the fruit. Nevertheless, it is worth persevering in order to reach some conclusions about the quality of the wine and how it might age.

 Fill up the glass once more and put it to one side. Taste it after an hour and then again later in the evening. Write notes on what you find each time.

You will probably find that the wine starts to open out and improve as more oxygen gets to it. Of course, this is a very crude

VINTAGE BOTTLE CELLAR AT CHATEAU LATOUR

experiment because you are not giving the wine time to go through all the complex changes that take place in a maturing bottle of wine, but it will give you some idea of what happens.

You might even want to leave the wine until the next day to see what happens when this process continues. By morning it may well be quite unpleasant to drink. When wine goes "over the hill" the tannins start to break up and the wine takes on a kind of gritty texture. The wine does not actually separate, but it no longer feels smooth and rounded in the mouth. If it oxidizes as well it will take on a flat aroma something like bad sherry.

MATURITY IN GREAT RED WINES

Given time, fine wines from the best vintages gradually evolve into delicious wines of great complexity. This may take five to ten years in the case of Chianti Classico Riserva and Rioja Gran Reserva or as long as twenty years in the case of the great estates of Bordeaux.

Lesser wines will be ready to drink much more quickly—perhaps in two to three years. These wines include ordinary Bordeaux, Chianti and Rioja Crianza and many of the middle-priced wines from other areas.

Pour a fresh glass of wine A, then wines B and C. Taste them in date order, starting with the youngest. Make a note on the color, aroma and palate.

Whichever vertical flight of wines you have chosen

DECANTING YOUNG WINE

It is sometimes possible to improve a wine that is not yet quite ready to drink by pouring it into a decanter to give it a little air. However, this really applies only to wines that are almost at their peak.

Very young wines, which need many years to mature, will not benefit from this treatment. The complex processes that take place during maturation cannot be simulated by an hour or so in contact with the air and you will get a very poor approximation of what the wine should be like. Indeed the better the wine the less it is likely to benefit from "breathing" in this way. Either it is ready or it is not.

There is no point in decanting everyday wines, which are ready to drink at an early age, or classic wines that have passed their peak. It will make no difference in the first case and will simply make matters worse in the second.

they should illustrate how good red wine matures over time. Depending on how much you have paid for your wines—a good wine is expensive to produce because of the time invested in creating it—you may find that even the oldest wine you have chosen is still rather young in terms of how far it has matured.

Look at your notes again and decide whether or not you think each wine is ready to drink.

A very young wine that is raw and unbalanced may need years to mature. If the wine is slightly unbalanced, with strong acidity and tannin, you might need to put it aside for one or two years. Conversely, a wine that is nearly in balance may only need six months to become very palatable indeed.

Remember that you may get an indication of the age and maturity of a wine by looking at the color, particularly on the rim of the wine. Deep purple colors tend to mature to deep brick. The first signs of these changes are visible on the rim of the wine, which starts to show a tinge of orange or light brown.

Your nose and palate should confirm your findings here. In a more mature wine the acids and tannins will be less obtrusive. The fruit should be coming through well and may take on a vegetal aroma. The wine will be mellow, with all the components blending together to create a balanced whole.

Discuss the wines with the other tasters if you are tasting in a group, and see if you can come to a consensus about the maturity of the wine. Remember to add this information to your notes when you transfer them to your notebook. It could come in useful in the future.

Have you considered the overall balance of those wines that you feel are ready to drink?

Balance is what both the winemaker and the wine connoisseur are seeking in their wines. A great wine is one in which all the components have married well and are in perfect harmony. This is fine wine at its peak. Luckily this is not usually a fleeting moment.

THE VINEYARD OF CASTELLO DEI RAMPOLLA IN CHIANTI, TUSCANY

The lifespan of a wine is a fairly gradual curve from a nearly mature wine, through its peak, to a gracefully aging one.

MATURITY IN GREAT WHITE WINES

The very best white wines evolve more quickly than red wines, so they are not matured in bottle or wood for as long. Some take just five to eight years to reach their peak, but there are exceptions. Sauternes from Bordeaux, Côteaux du Layon from the Loire and German wine at the Trockenbeere-nauslese level, for example, may take as long as fifteen to twenty years.

Pour wines D, E and F. Taste them in date order, starting with the youngest. Make a note on the color, aroma and palate.

The vertical flight of wines you have chosen should give you an idea of how good white wine matures over time. You would not expect the Meursault and Carneros wines to last quite as long as the others, but they should still show complex, honeyed aromas and flavors, which may include oak.

The Sauternes and Trockenbeerenauslese wines could well be affected by noble rot (see page 34). If so they will exhibit the characteristic raisiny, caramel aromas you may have experienced in Tasting 2. The best of these wines gain in complexity and interest without losing their balancing acidity.

The Côteaux du Layon wines of the Loire Valley are unusual in that the best can go on improving for twenty or even thirty years. They, too, take on wonderful aromas and flavors which are well balanced by natural acidity.

Look at your notes again and decide whether or not you think each wine is ready to drink.

Remember that you may get an indication of age and maturity by looking at the color of the wine. Good sweet wines, particularly, tend to darken as they mature. Your nose and palate will confirm your findings here. Great white wines grow in complexity, taking on wonderful aromas of lush dried fruits, nuts and caramel, without losing their acidity.

Discuss the wines with the other tasters and see if you can come to a consensus about the maturity of the wine. As before, remember to add this information when you transfer your comments to your notebook for future reference.

Have you considered the overall balance of those wines that you feel are ready to drink?

Balance is just as important in white wine as it is in red. In the best wines the fruit extract, sugar, acidity and oak (if present) blend to form a perfect whole.

THE IMPORTANCE OF VINTAGES

It is obviously important to know how old a wine is, but it is also essential to be familiar with the year in which it was harvested. Vintages reflect the weather of an area throughout the growing period and the effects that it has on the quality of the grapes and so of the wine.

Growers need just the right conditions for the vines to bloom and the fruit to set. They need rain and sunshine at the right time to ripen and fill the fruit. They do not want frost or hail at any time.

In the rare years when everything happens at the right time the growers produce a perfect crop that promises a great vintage. Grapes grown in these years

---

POOR VINTAGES

Generally speaking it is difficult to illustrate the importance of good and bad vintages in fine wine. If an older wine is still available today, it's because it was designed to last. Older wine from poor vintages will no longer be around to compare.

If you feel up to the difficulties of tasting *young* wines here are some suggestions for tasting poor vintages against the youngest of the red wines suggested for this tasting:

• Chianti Classico 1992

• Médoc 1992

• Pomerol 1991

• Rioja Reserva 1993

---

yield maximum fruit extract, and the wines made from them are rich and strong. These wines have much better aging potential than wines from lesser years.

Vintages are important for all levels of wine, but they increase in importance as you move up the quality scale. Top quality wines from the great wine-making estates of the world are made to be kept, and so must be able to withstand many years of maturation in cask or in bottle. Medium quality wines, too, improve if they are left to mature for a few years before being drunk.

Vintages are particularly important when buying fine wines from the classic areas of Europe. They are less important if you prefer the wines of America, Chile and Australia, where the weather varies less from year to year.

However, there have been disappointing vintages even in these areas. 1989 was not a very good year in California and 1992 and 1994 were bad for Australia, though Western Australia did somewhat better than the rest of the country in 1994.

Even with everyday wines it can be useful to know something about the vintage. For example, if you learn that Bordeaux or Burgundy is having a particularly good year, you would expect the lesser wines from those areas to be better than usual and might decide to buy a few to keep. Equally, if you learn that your favorite wine-producing region has had a bad vintage you might switch to buying wine from another area for a while.

By law, almost all European wines have to carry an indication of vintage. Exceptions are branded wines and those at the Vin de Table or Vin de Pays level or equivalent (see page 79). These wines will often be blends designed to eradicate the vagaries of the weather. They do not have any keeping potential and they should be drunk young. However, as the labels of blended wines carry no indication of their vintage they often remain on sale even when past their best.

There are few laws concerning the labeling of wines outside Europe, but wine-producers in America, Australia, Chile and elsewhere who wish their wines to compete with European wine do give an indication of the vintage on the label.

BUYING WINE "EN PRIMEUR"

Some wine merchants and importers offer their customers the opportunity to buy wine fine wine "en primeur." This means that you buy the wine before it is bottled and shipped. You pay the ex-cellar price (the price that is being asked by the producer) and the wine stays in casks or barrels in the producer's cellars until it is bottled. When the wine is shipped to your own country you will be asked to pay the cost of shipping the wine plus any taxes due on it.

The price of a first-class wine from a good vintage tends to go up after the vintage and buying en primeur offers a way to save money on such wines. However, problems have arisen when a merchant has gone into liquidation and the customer's title to the wine has not been formalized. This has usually meant that the customer has lost both the initial payment and the wine.

Talk to wine merchants or importers to see whether they offer the service as a matter of course, or if they will help you to buy in this way.

VINTAGE CHARTS

Vintage charts offer a useful resumé of the probable quality of wine from given areas in particular years. They may also give an indication of when the wines will be nearing maturity. This is obviously useful both for buying wine and for deciding when to drink it.

It is often quite difficult to decide how good a vintage really is. Reports pour out from the various wine-growing regions after the harvest. The problem is that no grower ever confesses to having a really bad year—though he may claim that his neighbors have!

Independent reports are not much better. "Vintages of the century" are announced frequently, but the wines do not always live up to expectations. Wines from so-called bad years can also prove to be much better than predicted.

All vintage charts should be treated with caution because the assessments in them are very general. Ideally they should be updated on a regular basis as initial ideas about the vintage are modified by observations of how the wine is actually progressing.

Even the best vintage charts give only a broad indication of the average level of quality. Individual wines may be much better—or much worse—than others. You really need to know your grower in order to make an accurate appraisal.

Complete the tasting by checking through your mnemonic, making full notes on the color, nose and palate of each wine. On the nose use your mnemonic for CGFIWM. On the palate remember FSATBBF. Transfer your notes to the notebook.

WHAT'S IN A NAME?

If you like a wine, study the label. Do not just make a note of the grape variety or the region it comes from, add the names of the winemaker or blender and bottler. This information can be just as important as the name of the region because the decisions taken by these people can make a real difference to the flavor of the wine in the bottle.

In most European wine-producing countries the wines are classified according to their region of origin. In all these regions the cultivation of grapes and their subsequent conversion into wine is subject to stringent wine laws. Often colloquially known as "appellation" laws, these rules and regulations were developed in France and are followed to a greater or lesser degree in the other wine-producing countries of Europe.

There are fewer wine regulations in the rest of the world, though most countries do insist that wine labels reflect what is in the bottle. In America and certain parts of Australia there is a move towards geographical labeling similar to that used in France. The criteria for such labeling are far less strict.

Once you know where a wine comes from you will begin to have some idea of what it will taste like. But the geographical factors, such as soil and climate, and the grape varieties used are not the whole story. Even in areas with strict wine-making laws, the winemaker often has a great deal of leeway in deciding exactly what kind of wine he wants to make.

Skill and experience are also very important, and you may well find that you enjoy one producer's wine much more than another's producer, even though the vineyards may be next door to each other.

This tasting concentrates on changes in the quality and style of wine as you progress through the classifications and up the price range. It also looks at the differences in style between wines at the same quality and price levels.

For A, B and C choose one of the suggested flights. The wines should come from the same vintage, the same region, and be made by the same producer. For D, E and F buy three wines from the same vintage and the same region, but from different producers. Make sure that they have the same apellation or, if there is no classification system in place, that they

---

THE WINES

A, B AND C

VIN DE TABLE ROUGE,
VIN DE PAYS D'OC AND
COTEAUX DU LANGUEDOC AC

ROSSO DI TOSCANA IGT,
ROSSO DI MONTALCINO DOC
AND
BRUNELLO DI MONTALCINO
DOCG

BERIECH NIERSTEINER QBA,
NIERSTEINER KABINETT QMP*
AND
NIERSTEINER SPÄTLESE QMP

WINES D, E AND F

MUSCADET AC*

NAPA VALLEY CHARDONNAY*

NEW ZEALAND SAUVIGNON
BLANC*

MEDOC AC*

CHIANTI CLASSICO DOCG*

EASTERN EUROPEAN CABERNET
SAUVIGNON*

SONOMA VALLEY CABERNET
SAUVIGNON*

*You may have some of these wines left
from previous tastings.

---

are priced at about the same level. Follow the Eight Steps to Tasting Wine set out at the beginning of Tasting 1 and use your mnemonics to make sure that you write a note on all aspects of the color, nose and palate of each wine.

THE IMPORTANCE OF GEOGRAPHICAL NAMES IN EUROPE

Most wine classification systems are based on the French system. Here the vineyards and wine regions are classified purely by geography and not, as many people suppose, by quality. Wines with the top classifications may be superior to those with a lower classification but this is not always so. Nor do all wines within the same classification reach the same standards of excellence.

The French appellation laws are specific to particular regions and guarantee the origin of a wine. They are designed to preserve what the French consider to be typical of a region. The laws define the precise vineyard areas (determined according to soil and aspect), the permitted grape varieties, maximum yields and the minimum level of alcohol in the wine. They may also

THE VILLAGE OF PAUILLAC PRODUCES A BORDEAUX SECOND GROWTH

FRENCH APPELLATION LAWS

Two hundred years ago French wines were so successful that the temptation to imitate them was very great. Fraudulently labeled wines appeared and the great names were in danger of becoming debased. Because of this the French authorities worked out a system of guaranteeing the origin of their wines. They started in 1855 with the great châteaux of the Médoc and Sauternes in Bordeaux and the classification laws have changed very little since then.

cover vineyard and cellar practices.

The best wines of France, which must come from one of the specially designated regions, are awarded an Appellation d'Origine Contrôlée (AC). These wines now account for nearly a quarter of all French wines.

The designated regions may be as large as Bordeaux or as small as Bandol. The larger regions often contain smaller demarcated regions which are considered to have an even better potential to produce good wine. Thus Margaux AC is a designated village within the Bordeaux sub-region of Haut-Médoc AC.

Vin Délimité de Qualité Supérieure (VDQS) is the

second category or level with similar rules to those for AC wines. This is a rapidly shrinking category because the wines are promoted to AC as soon as they are good enough.

Vin de Pays wines were introduced in 1965 and now represent about 14 percent of French wine. The idea was to give regional definition to wines that would otherwise have gone to be blended into ordinary Vin de Table. The designated regions at this level are quite large.

The rules for Vin de Pays wines follow the same guidelines as the AC laws but are less stringent, allowing higher yields, different grape varieties and lower alcohol levels. There is more scope for the winemaker to experiment with the type of wine he is making.

Table wine or Vin de Table accounts for all the rest. These are the "vin ordinaires" of the regions, though Vin de Table wine can actually come from anywhere in France. A great deal of surplus table wine

ITALIAN VINO DA TAVOLA SPECIALS

A few years ago some leading Italian wine-producers, rebelling against the limitations of the local DOC wine laws, decided to make first-class wine in their own way. Because they were no longer adhering to the wine laws they could only label their wine Vino da Tavola, but there was nothing to prevent their charging a high price for it. These so-called "Super Tuscans" have done so well that they are accepted as being some of the best in the world. Well-known examples are Tignanello and Sassicaia.

is turned into grape brandy or industrial alcohol.

In practice the AC system means that grapes grown outside an AC or Vin de Pays area can be used only to make Vin de Table. On the other hand grapes grown within an AC area can, provided the winemaker abides by the wine laws of that area, be used to make whichever level of wine the grower wishes.

Thus in Bordeaux a winemaker on an estate in Listrac could make Margaux AC, Médoc AC or Bordeaux AC. He will probably chose to make Margaux AC because the name itself commands a higher price than the other levels of wine.

If, on the other hand, the winemaker is based in the less well-known Languedoc region he may chose to make Vin de Pays d'Oc rather than a Côteaux de Languedoc AC because the more flexible Vin de Pays wine laws allow him to make a more interesting wine that might be easier to sell.

In general, as you move up the scale from Vin de Table and its counterparts to appellation contrôlée and its equivalents, you will pay more for the wine. Due to the stricter laws controlling their production, the quality of the wine may also improve, but this is by no means always the case.

However, at AC level there should be fewer of the thin and not very fruity white wines or harsh tannic red wines that are sometimes found at the lowest level and more wines with good fruit, interesting flavors and some complexity.

CLASSIFICATIONS OF FINE WINES IN FRANCE

In France the regions of Bordeaux, Burgundy, Champagne and Alsace have devised classification pro-

EUROPEAN CLASSIFICATION SYSTEMS

Here are the titles and abbreviations of the different levels in some of the classification systems of Europe. They are listed in descending order of quality. The numbered levels are not equivalents. Thus Italian DOC is not the same as French VDQS.

FRANCE:

1. Appellation d'Origine Contrôlée or AC (occasionally AOC)
2. Vins Délimités de Qualité Supérieure or VDQS
3. Vins de Pays
4. Vins de Table

See opposite for the extra classifications for Bordeaux, Burgundy, Champagne and Alsace.

ITALY:

A new classification system is being introduced in Italy which is designed to try to guarantee both origin and quality. Thus if a grower in a DOCG area makes a wine that does not come up to DOCG standards he can have it classified as DOC or IGT on a kind of sliding scale. He does not have to specify in advance which wine he is going to make.

1. Denominazione di Origine Controllata e Garantita (DOCG)
2. Denominazione di Origine Controllata (DOC)
3. Indicazioni Geografiche Tipiche (IGT)
4. Vino da Tavola

SPAIN:

1. Denominación de Origen Calificada (DOCa)
2. Denominación de Origen (DO)
3. Vino de Mesa

PORTUGAL:

1. Denominação de Origem controlada (DOC)
2. Indicação de Proveniência Regulamentada (IPR)
3. Vinho Regional
4. Vinho de Mesa

Regiões Demarcadas used to be the top classification in Portugal and you will still see this designation on labels from Portugal.

GERMANY:

Germany has a double-barreled classification system. There is a regional classification system and a quality system based on sugar levels in the grape must.

Regional Classifications:

1. Einzellagen: Individual vineyards
2. Grosslagen: 152 groups of vineyards from several villages
3. Bereiche: 34 broad groupings of villages
4. Anbaugebiete: 11 large wine regions

Quality Classifications:

1. Qualitätswein mit Prädikat (QmP). The classifications within this category are given on page 28.
2. Qualitätswein bestimmter Anbaugebiete (QbA)
3. Landwein
4. Deutscher Tafelwein

cedures over and above the AC system. The vineyards with the very best soils and aspects are placed at the top of the pyramid, those with less favorable conditions come further down.

In Bordeaux both the Médoc and St-Emilion have their own classification systems. The Médoc, which takes in the entire region north from Bordeaux to Soulac, has two appellations—Médoc AC in the north and Haut-Médoc AC in the south. In the Haut-Médoc there are six villages—Margaux, Moulis, St-Julien, St-Estèphe, Listrac and Pauillac—which may use their own names. The estates within these villages are then classified into First Growths or Premiers Crus Classés (the top level), through Second, Third, Fourth and Fifth Growths to Crus Bourgeois. These rankings have not changed since 1855.

St-Emilion is the overall AC in this area, which covers a large part of the north bank of the Dordogne. Here the estates are classified into Premiers Grand Crus Classés (the top level), Grands Crus Classés and Grands Crus. These ranking are much more recent as they are reassessed every ten years.

In Burgundy the system is based on an appraisal of vineyards rather than on an assessment of individual estates. Grands Crus are the very top vineyards. These are followed by Premiers Crus or second level vineyards. The top wines of Champagne are classified in the same manner, but here it is the villages rather than the vineyards that are awarded Grand Cru or Premier Cru standing.

Until recently all the wines of Alsace have been classified and labeled by grape variety rather than by estates or vineyards. Now, new legislation has defined a small number of specific vineyards that are allowed to identify themselves as Grands Crus.

Pour wines A, B and C. Taste the wines in the order in which they are listed and write notes on all aspects of the color, nose and palate.

The wines for this tasting represent the steps in the wine hierarchy for a variety of European countries. These are wines that have been made for export and you are unlikely to encounter any really bad examples.

TASTING SUGGESTION

If you like the white wines of Burgandy, you might like to taste a flight of wines from Chablis. Choose a Petit Chablis AC, a Chablis AC, and a Chablis Premier Cru AC. If possible taste wines from the same vintage and the same producer.

The wines of Chablis are made from the Chardonnay grape variety and are characteristically fresh with flinty or steely fruit. Some wines are matured in oak barrels, others are not. Expect the Petit Chablis to be simple and straightforward. Check that all the components are in balance and that there is a pleasant finish.

The Chablis AC should offer a greater depth of flavor and a little more complexity. However, there are many Chablis wines on the market that do not justify the premium prices they command.

The Chablis Premier Cru should offer more character, concentration of fruit and possibly oaky flavors. These wines are much fuller and more complex than their juniors.

If you have chosen the French flight of wines expect the Vin de Table to be very straightforward and without complexity. You should find a reasonable level of fruit, but it is unlikely that you will be able to identify a specific grape variety. If there are no rough edges in the form of excessive acidity or tannin you will be doing quite well!

The Vin de Pays d'Oc area takes in Languedoc-Roussillon. The wines, like other wines at this level, can be very drinkable. Whether you have chosen a blend or a single varietal wine such as Cabernet Sauvignon or Syrah/Shiraz you should find plenty of fruity flavors, but do not expect a great deal of complexity. These wines are designed to be drunk young and do not usually develop much in the way of secondary vegetal or spicy flavors.

The Côteaux de Languedoc area takes in 121 villages of which 11 are now allowed to add their own names to the AC name. Two villages that have recently been elevated are La Clape and Cabrières. Some winemakers use oak barrels to mature the wine, which can then age in bottle very successfully for several years. Thus your notes on this wine will depend upon which style of wine you happen to have.

If you have chosen the Italian flight of wines you should also experience a very definite increase in quality and complexity as you move up the appellation scale. These wines are interesting because, unlike the Languedoc wines, they are all based on the same grape variety—Sangiovese.

Rosso di Toscana IGT is roughly similar in quality to French Vin de Pays wine and may come from anywhere in Tuscany. If it is a good example it will be firm but fruity with good acidity and tannin. The Italians respect these qualities, and this wine will probably be more complex than its French equivalent. However, if it is not such a good example it may be lacking in fruit.

The Rosso di Montalcino DOC wine comes from a small area in the southwestern corner of Tuscany. Expect to find plenty of fresh plummy fruit with balancing tannins and acidity. The wine can be sold after a year and is not intended to last for a great deal longer, but it can take on some interesting cinnamon spice flavors as it matures.

Brunello di Montalcino DOCG is a serious, slow-maturing wine that needs several years of maturation in wood before it is bottled. It is not sold until it is at least four years old. Brunello refers to the grape variety which is a type of Sangiovese. Expect a rich wine with deep intensity of all flavors. If you have a good example the fruit should still be around to

THE LANGUAGE OF LABELS

SPAIN

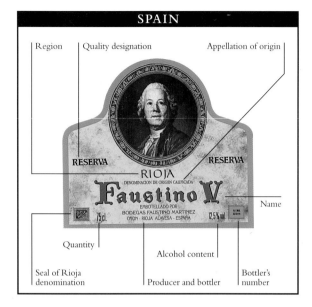

Region

Quality designation

Appellation of origin

RESERVA   RESERVA

RIOJA
DENOMINACION DE ORIGEN CALIFICADA
Faustino V
EMBOTELLADO POR:
BODEGAS FAUSTINO MARTINEZ
OYON · RIOJA ALAVESA · ESPAÑA
75 cl.   12,5 % vol.

Name

Quantity

Alcohol content

Seal of Rioja
denomination

Producer and bottler

Bottler's
number

FRANCE/BURGUNDY

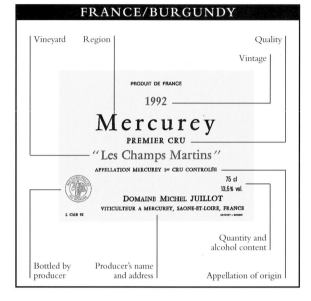

Vineyard   Region

Quality

Vintage

PRODUIT DE FRANCE

1992

Mercurey

PREMIER CRU

"Les Champs Martins"

APPELLATION MERCUREY 1er CRU CONTROLÉE

75 cl
13,5% vol.

DOMAINE MICHEL JUILLOT
VITICULTEUR A MERCUREY, SAONE-ET-LOIRE, FRANCE
L CMB 92

Bottled by
producer

Producer's name
and address

Quantity and
alcohol content

Appellation of origin

GERMANY

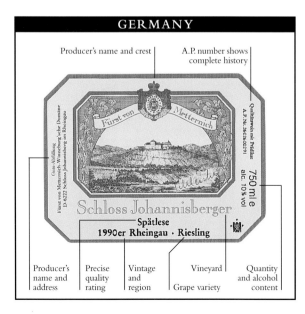

Producer's name and crest

A.P. number shows
complete history

Fürst von Metternich

Qualitätswein mit Prädikat
A.P. Nr. 26026/002/91

Guts-Abfüllung
Fürst von Metternich-Winneburg'sche Domäne
D-6222 Schloss Johannisberg im Rheingau

750 ml e
alc. 10% vol.

Schloss Johannisberger

Spätlese
1990er Rheingau · Riesling

Producer's
name and
address

Precise
quality
rating

Vintage
and
region

Grape variety

Vineyard

Quantity
and alcohol
content

ITALY

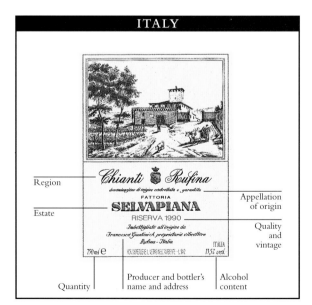

Chianti Rufina

FATTORIA
SELVAPIANA
RISERVA 1990

Imbottigliato all'origine da
Francesco Giuntini A. proprietario viticoltore
Rufina - Italia

750 ml e   ITALIA
13,5% vol.

Region

Estate

Appellation
of origin

Quality
and
vintage

Quantity

Producer and bottler's
name and address

Alcohol
content

FRANCE/CHAMPAGNE

Producer's name

Region

Brand name

Quantity

Producer and bottler's address

Code number showing producer's status

Style

Alcohol content

CHILE

Producer and bottler's name

Vintage

Producer's name

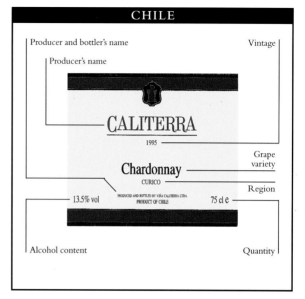

Grape variety

Region

Alcohol content

Quantity

U.S.A.

Winery name

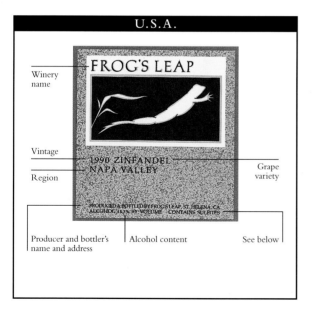

Vintage

Region

Grape variety

Producer and bottler's name and address

Alcohol content

See below

AUSTRALIA

Producer's name

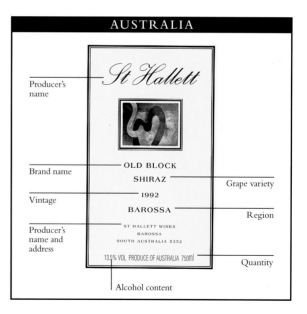

Brand name

Vintage

Producer's name and address

Grape variety

Region

Quantity

Alcohol content

balance the heavy woods and tannins. Look for the characteristic pepper, cinnamon, and tea aromas and flavors of the mature wine. If you have difficulty finding the Italian wines suggested you could taste a reasonably priced Vino da Tavola wine before the Rosso Toscana and substitute a Chianti Classico DOCG for the Brunello. You might also like to add one of the special Vini da Tavola. You will recognize them by their high price. Taste this after the other three.

If you have chosen the German flight of white wines you should not only find wines of increasing quality and complexity, but also of increasing sweetness because the German classification of wines is based on the sugar content of the grape must as well as on geographical area.

Most German wines are fruity and relatively sweet so you will need to concentrate on the intensity and complexity of flavor of each wine when judging their quality. Think about whether the sweetness is balanced by the acidity.

TASTING SUGGESTION

Just as European wines tend to cost more as you move up the classification levels, the more a new world wine costs, the better it should be.

If you would like to try this kind of tasting with American wines taste a branded wine such as Gallo California White or Fetzer "Chablis," followed by a middle-price Chardonnay wine from the Sonoma or Napa Valley and a more expensive Chardonnay wine from the same area.

Expect the Qba wine to have very simple easy-drinking fruit. The actual flavors may not be very specific. On the other hand it may be lightly flowery or have a herbaceous, lemony aroma. Good examples will not be too cloying and should have a reasonably fresh finish.

Wines at the Kabinett level should be fuller and have more complicated aromas and flavors. Depending on the grape varieties used you may find more definite varietal aromas. This wine will probably be more interesting to drink. Did you notice the difference in the sweetness levels?

Once you get to the Spätlese level you can expect quite complex well-balanced wines with a good finish. This wine will be sweeter again, but should have good balancing acidity. If you have chosen a Riesling expect to find plenty of grapefruity flavors in a young wine and oily, gasoline aromas in a more mature wine. Your sample may be affected by noble rot, but it is not very likely at this level.

Look at your notes again and use them to sum up each wine in a few simple words. Your conclusions will help to remind you of the kind of wine to expect at that classification level and from that region. For example, you might describe the French Vin de Table as "fruity but thin and rather acidic," the Rosso di Montalcino as "good drinkable wine with plenty of fruit—serve with pasta," and the German Spätlese wine as "unexpectedly lush with oily fruit and a long finish." Do not forget to record whether you liked each wine or not.

MARESH VINEYARDS TASTING ROOM, OREGON

FINE WINE

The term "fine wine" is simply shorthand for a wine of the very best quality from one of the classic wine-making areas of the world. The classic areas or wines were traditionally considered to be Bordeaux, Burgundy, Champagne, the Loire, the upper Rhône and Alsace in France; the Mosel and Rheingau in Germany; Barolo and Chianti in Italy; Rioja and Jerez in Spain and the Douro Valley in Portugal. Today this informal list must be widened to include the best Californian and Australian regions.

As time goes on classic wines may well come from some of the emerging wine-making regions such as Washington State, the Ribeiro del Douro in Spain, and Chile.

WINE CLASSIFICATION SYSTEMS IN THE NEW WORLD

In America and most other so-called new world wine regions, the situation is very different from that of Europe. Until recently there were no classification systems at all. Winemakers in the Napa Valley in California, for example, labeled their wines with reference to California, the Napa Valley, the local town, the name of the winery or vineyard, their own name, or any other name they chose. The same was true in other states and in Australia and New Zealand.

As a result names like "Chablis" and "Burgundy" were given to wines which bore no relationship to their European counterparts. These names, of course, could not be used on wines made for export as they are protected in their own countries. It was also necessary to explain to foreign consumers what they could expect from bottles labeled with vineyard and producer names with which they were unfamiliar. The situation gave rise to a new system of naming wines in America.

The solution was to use the names of the grape varieties on the labels of quality wines. These became known as "varietal" wines and the idea was taken up in Australia, New Zealand and Chile. It is now also being used by the emerging wine-producing countries of eastern Europe such as Hungary, Moldova and the Czech Republic.

The authorities in most wine-producing countries also insist that the wine labels give a reasonable reflection of what is in the bottle, though in some countries there is a good deal of flexibility. In California, for example, a varietal wine labeled "Chardonnay" or

"Cabernet Sauvignon" must contain at least 75 percent of the named grape variety. In Oregon, a "Chardonnay" must contain 90 percent of that grape variety, but a "Cabernet Sauvignon" that is blended with its traditional Bordeaux partners of Merlot and Cabernet Franc, can contain 75 percent of the named variety.

Pour wines D, E and F. Taste the wines in any order and write notes on all aspects of the color, nose and palate. How much difference is there between them?

These three wines were made under the same appellation laws, in the same region and in the same year, but by different producers. Within the appellation laws

NÉGOCIANTS

A *négociant* is a merchant who buys wine from smaller growers and producers and blends and bottles it under his own name. Georges Duboeuf in the Beaujolais is one of the best-known *négociants*.

The *négociant's* name may be prominent on the label or it may lie in the small print at the base. For example, instead of stating *mis en bouteille au château* or *au domaine*, (bottled on the property where it was made), the label might say *mis en bouteille par Monsieur X*. In this case the wine was bottled by Mr. X at his premises, wherever he happens to be based.

Négociants are becoming less important as the smaller growers begin to sell their own wine directly to buyers from other areas or from abroad.

each producer made different decisions about the allowed grapes to grow, the blend of grapes to use in the wine, wine-making techniques and the maturation method. These decisions affect the style and taste of the wine.

The only way to be sure of finding what you like in the future is to remember the names of those producers who make your preferred style of wine. This becomes even more important when there are fewer rules and regulations surrounding the way the wine is made. In the new world, wineries can and do make wine very different in style from their neighbors'.

Discuss each wine and your reactions to it with the other tasters. Are there any marked differences in the fruit, acidity or tannin levels of the three wines? If you were tasting the wines blind do you think that you would say there was an affinity between them or would you guess they were from different regions?

How do you think the wines have been matured— are they woody or oaky and if so is this an attractive feature or not? Are the wines balanced and in harmony, or do they have rough edges? Do you like or dislike any of the wines? If there is a back label on any of the bottles, read it as it may help you to interpret what you are tasting.

Are the wines ready to drink? Do you think that they would benefit by being drunk with food?

Complete the tasting by checking through your mnemonic, making full notes on the color, nose and palate of each wine. On the nose use your mnemonic for CGFIWM. On the palate remember FSATBBF. Transfer your notes to the notebook.

THINK PINK!

Rosé wines are sometimes dismissed as colored white wines or weak red wines. This is a pity because good rosé wines can be very enjoyable. At their best they are delicious wines to drink on a summer's day and fun wines to drink at a party. Of course, not all rosé wines are of high quality, so it is worth making an effort to search out a few reliable examples.

Rosé wine is usually made from the common red grape varieties such as Cabernet Sauvignon, Cabernet Franc, Pinot Noir, Gamay, Grenache, Sangiovese and Merlot. Crushing and fermentation are begun in the same way as for red wine (see page 116), but the fermenting must is separated from the skins after a few days to prevent it from taking on too much color. Whether a rosé wine is very pale or quite deep in color will depend upon the type of grapes used and the length of time that the must remains on the skins. The color of rosé wine does not tell you very much about the grape variety.

Rosé wines do not vary as much in their range of tastes and flavors as either red or white wines, but there are definite varietal differences and they do vary quite a lot in their sweetness and alcohol levels. They are intended to be drunk young and do not usually have any aging potential.

Rosé wines are produced in most of the viticultural regions of Europe, but fewer are made in the new world. Where producers do make rosé wines they often make a range of styles, so you will find a selection of dry, medium and sweet wines, as well as sparkling wines.

This tasting concentrates on the difference between rosé wines from various parts of Europe. If you would like to add an American rosé wine to the tasting look for Bonny Doon Vin Gris de Cigare rosé or Sierra Vista Belle Rosé.

Think about the same elements you would when tasting red or white wines. Follow the Eight Steps to Tasting Wine set out at the beginning of Tasting 1.

Pour wines A, B, C and D. Begin by comparing the color and appearance of the wines. Check that they are clear and bright, then make a note on the depth and type of color.

Very pale wines tend to have light or delicate aromas and flavors. As the color deepens, so does the taste. Very delicate wines can have quite complex flavors, but they are often rather boring.

The color of rosé wine may vary from pale roses and pinks or even pale orange

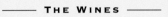

THE WINES

A. FRENCH VIN DE PAYS ROSE

B. SPANISH ROSADO
from Rioja or Navarra

C. FRENCH CLAIRET OR ROSE
from Bordeaux

D. FRENCH TAVEL ROSE
from the Rhône Valley

through salmon pink and coral to strong reddish hues. Some rosé wines, such as those from Rioja in Spain, could almost be mistaken for red. If your rosé shows brick and brown colors, it is probably too old and past its best.

Taste the wines, making a note on their aromas.

Do strawberries, raspberries, black cherries, black currants or blackberries figure in your notes? You will now begin to gain a better idea of the grape varieties used to make a rosé wine.

The French Vin de Pays wine may have been made from any number of grape varieties. Those made in the South of France from Grenache often have a blackberry aroma; those using Cabernet Sauvignon grapes may be reminiscent of black currants. Do not worry if you cannot identify any specific fruit aromas, simply note whether or not the wine smells fruity.

The predominant red grape varieties in Rioja and Navarra are Tempranillo and Garnacha Tinta (Grenache in France). Both these grape varieties give a really fresh, fruity, even jammy flavor to rosé wines with raspberry and strawberry overtones. Expect a high degree of intensity—these are wines with character.

The Bordeaux grape

varieties are quite different. Cabernet Sauvignon, Merlot and Cabernet Franc are much more likely to give plum or black currant aromas. Expect stronger smells if you have a Clairet rather than a rosé wine. "Clairet" is the term used in Bordeaux to distinguish a dark pink or pale red rosé from a light rosé.

Tavel Rosé is the only wine made in an area to the west of Orange on the lower Rhône in France. Expect a heady aroma of warm, dusty cherries.

Do you detect any woody or vanilla aromas in any of the wines? The Spanish wine may well have spent some time in new oak barrels so you might expect to find some vanilla on the nose. The Clairet and the Tavel may have seen a little wood, but it is unlikely to have been new oak. The most you will find is a little pepper or spiciness.

THE HILLTOP TOWN OF LAGUARDIA IN RIOJA

Take another sip of each wine and make full notes on the palate and finish. Begin by checking whether the palate confirms what you found on the nose.

Are the fruity and woody flavors more pronounced on the palate than on the nose?

LANCERS AND MATEUS ROSE

Lancers and Mateus Rosé are branded wines produced by the Portuguese companies of Fonseca and Sogrape. A variety of local grapes from four or five different regions of Portugal are blended to taste the same every year. Expect a sherbet, peardrops or candy aroma and a very light sugary taste.

Now check the sweetness and acidity levels of the wines. Can you place them in ascending order of sweetness?

Despite its full and definite flavor the Spanish wine is likely to be the driest but, unless you have chosen something very unusual, it will be closely followed by the Clairet and the Vin de Pays wine. Discuss your findings with the other tasters if you are tasting with a group. The Tavel Rosé is a much sweeter wine. Is it balanced by good acidity?

Make a note on the tannin and alcohol levels of each wine and their overall balance.

Very light rosé wines from Vin de Pays regions do not usually contain very much tannin. They are also relatively low in alcohol and so are quite light. The rosé wines from Bordeaux and Spain, on the other hand, may well contain a small amount of tannin. Alcohol levels will be around 11 to 12 percent by volume, resulting in relatively medium-bodied wines.

   As well as being fairly sweet, Tavel Rosé has a high alcohol content and with its depth of fruit and spice is a fairly heavy wine—particularly for a rosé.

Complete the tasting by checking through your mnemonic, making full notes on the color, nose and palate of each wine. On the nose use your mnemonic for CGFIWM. On the palate remember FSATBBF. Transfer your notes to the notebook.

BLUSH WINES

Blush wines or White Zinfandel were developed in California as a way to use excess red Zinfandel grapes. These are crushed and the skins immediately removed from the juice, which is then fermented to produce an almost, but not quite, white wine that is usually fairly sweet. The wine is called "Blush" because it retains a touch of pink.

   Blush wines initially enjoyed enormous popularity in America, prompting winemakers to use other red grape varieties to swell the production and meet demand from other parts of the world. One or two wine-producing regions in Europe attempted to copy the Americans, but have given up as the first flush of popularity faded away.

TASTING SUGGESTION

If you cannot find all of the wines suggested for this tasting substitute one of the following European wines instead.
• Gris de Gris
• Anjou Rosé or other rosé wines from the Loire Valley
• Lirac from the lower Rhône
• Bergerac Rosé, Cabernet d'Anjou Rosé, Cabernet de Saumur Rosé or Provence Rosé
• Bardolino Chiaretto or Rosato wine

BRING ON THE BUBBLES

Champagne is *the* celebration wine. It signifies triumph, success and special occasions. In fact, it has become so synonymous with celebration that people tend to regard any sparkling wine served at special occasions as "champagne." However, true Champagne comes only from a small area of northeastern France around Rheims and Epernay.

There have been many attempts to copy Champagne, and almost every wine-producing area now has its own sparkling wine. Many of these wines are made in the same way as Champagne, with the second fermentation which produces the bubbles taking place in the bottle, but they do not taste the same. They used to be labeled *Méthode Champenoise*, but the French have successfully limited the use of that phrase to Champagne alone.

Among those who have sought to make first-class sparkling wine outside the Champagne region are the Champagne houses themselves. A number of them have set up wine-making operations in California, Australia and New Zealand, choosing sites that are well suited to growing the same grape varieties as those used in Champagne. With these grapes and their expertise they are creating first-class sparkling wines that, in some cases, are beginning to rival the French originals.

Sparkling wines made in the traditional Champagne manner can be found in other parts of France such as the Loire Valley, Burgundy and Alsace; in Spain, where this wine is known as Cava, and in America, Australia, New Zealand and South Africa. Like Champagne, the wines may be dry, medium or sweet, and white or rosé.

A more economical way of producing sparkling wines is the *cuve close* or closed tank method. Here the bubbles are produced through secondary fermentation in large tanks. The wines are bottled later. This much cheaper way of producing sparkling wine is used to make "Sekt," sparkling wine from Germany. The wines are usually quite pleasant but not memorable.

The very cheapest sparkling wine is made by forcing carbon dioxide into ordinary wine. There is no secondary fermentation at all. These wines are rarely successful as the base wine is usually inferior and the bubbles do not last long.

This tasting looks at the difference between Champagne and other sparkling wine, and at the range of choice available. If possible, for A and B choose wines made by the same Champagne house, such as Mumm/Mumm Cuvée Napa, Deutz/Domaine Deutz, Taittinger/Domaine Carneros, Moët & Chandon/Domaine Chandon, Piper

---

THE WINES

A. A GOOD NON-VINTAGE CHAMPAGNE BRUT
from France

B. A PREMIUM DRY SPARKLING WINE
made by one of the French Champagne houses in California

C. SPANISH CAVA

D. FRENCH CREMANT DE LOIRE, CREMANT D'ALSACE OR CREMANT DE BOURGOGNE

E. A SPARKLING WINE
made by local producers in the traditional way from America, Australia or New Zealand

F. ASTI SPUMANTE
from Italy

Heidsieck/Piper Sonoma, Pommery and Lanson/Scharffenberger, and Roederer/Roederer Estate. If you choose Deutz you may be able to organize a three-way tasting by adding Sparkling Maison Deutz from New Zealand to the other two. Think about the same elements as when tasting red or white wines. Follow the Eight Steps to Tasting Wine set out at the beginning of Tasting 1.

IS CHAMPAGNE REALLY UNIQUE?

Can you taste the difference between true Champagne and sparkling wines made in other parts of the world? Until quite recently the answer to this question would have been a resounding yes. Today, not even the experts are always able tell which is which.

Champagne is made from a blend of wines made from different grape varieties grown in a cool climate in strictly classified vineyards on a particular type of chalky soil. Non-vintage Champagne is blended from the wines of a number of different vintages to produce a consistent taste every year. The way in which the bubbles are produced and the wine matured and cleared is comparatively long and complex. All these factors contribute to its very special taste.

Pour wines A and B and taste them in that order. Tasting sparkling wine is much the same as tasting still wine, so start with the color.

These wines are both made in association with the same French Champagne house, one in Champagne itself and the other in California. They have both been made using the traditional Champagne method of inducing the secondary fermentation in the bottle.

Champagne is usually pale straw or pale yellow in color. The California wine may have a little more depth of color, but is unlikely to be very different. As both these wines mature, their color will deepen to pale gold.

Now look at the size and behavior of the bubbles.

The bubbles in both wines should be small and neat and rise in a steady, continuous stream. Sparkling wines that have not been made in the traditional Champagne manner tend to have larger bubbles which disappear more quickly.

OPENING SPARKLING WINE

Take care when opening sparkling wine as the contents are under pressure and the cork could come flying out with disastrous results. Keep your thumb pressed over the top of the cork as you ease it out—you do not have to make a great pop.

How would you describe the aroma of each wine? Take care when sniffing sparkling wine—the bubbles can get up your nose if you put it too close to the wine!

Have you used words like "fruity and fresh" or "dried yeast," "apples," "nutty," or "biscuity"? Champagne houses vary in the type of wine they produce, with some going for a soft fruity character, others for a more aggressive, nutty style.

Young Champagne can have a slightly fresh yeasty aroma, often with appley fruit. Older wines tend towards more mellow, toasty or dried yeast aromas and you may have used words such as smoky, caramel, or even meaty.

Most Champagne is not released for sale until it is at least fifteen months old and it continues to improve if it is allowed to mature for a further two or even three years. Non-vintage Champagne can be drunk as soon as it is released, but it will almost always improve if you keep it for six months to a year. Do not store it for more than two years as the corks in non-vintage Champagne are not designed to last much longer than that. If the cork goes, the wine will spoil.

Champagne has a high level of acidity and this may well come through on the nose in the form of tart fruit aromas. If the wine is young it may need time for the acidity to settle down. Do not expect to find any wood aromas or vanilla. Champagne is matured in bottle not in cask. However, a few brands of Champagne may contain wines in the blend that have been fermented, though not stored, in oak casks.

This can give an even more biscuity character than usual to the wine.

Unlike most other white wines, Champagne is made from both red and white grape varieties. They are the white Chardonnay, and the red Pinot Noir and Pinot Meunier. Very often wines made from the different grape varieties are blended together, so you may not be able to distinguish any particular varietal character.

However, some wines are made with Chardonnay alone (labeled Blanc de Blanc) or with Pinot Noir

RIPE PINOT NOIR GRAPES

VINTAGE CHAMPAGNE

In good years, the Champagne producers may "declare a vintage." This means that instead of blending wines from a number of different years, as is the case for non-vintage Champagne, they make the wine from selected grapes from that year alone. These wines are not usually released until three years after they are made. Ideally they need at least five years' maturation. They are much fuller and more complex than non-vintage wines.

Some Champagne houses also produce an extra-special luxury Champagne. Examples are Dom Pérignon from Moët & Chandon, Bollinger Cuvée Année, Pol Roger Cuvée Churchill, Roederer Cristal and Krug Grande Cuvée. Some of these wines are described as "recently disgorged" or RD for short. This means that the wine has spent much more time on its yeast deposit before being disgorged and bottled. As a result the wines have more depth and are more toasty or biscuity in character.

alone (labeled Blanc de Noir). The latter tend to be coarser and more aggressive than the creamy and lightly toasty Blanc de Blancs.

The California wine (wine B) has been made from the same grape varieties and in the same way as the Champagne. How do the aromas compare? Can you detect similar fresh yeast and appley aromas, or are there nutty and toasty ones? If you had not seen the label do you think that you might have thought wine B was a true French Champagne?

Now take a sip of each wine, sucking in a little air each time if you can. This is more difficult to do with sparkling wine than with still wine. Make full notes on the palate of both wines.

Check whether your impression of the style of the wines is confirmed on the palate. Do they seem as

THE MONTAGNE DE RHEIMS, CHAMPAGNE

CREMANT WINES

Crémant means creamy, and the term originated in the Champagne area where wines labeled *crémant* were under less pressure than regular Champagne. Today the term is used to refer to fully sparkling French wine made by the *Méthode Champenoise* outside the Champagne area. The bubbles will usually be as aggressive as in any other sparkling wine.

young or as mature as they did on the nose? Is the acidity still very raw or has it mellowed? Do the wines taste as nutty or biscuity as they smelled? If the wines seemed similar on the nose, do they still seem so on the palate?

How dry or sweet do you think the wines are? Brut Champagne is very dry indeed and is usually rated at 1 on the European sweetness/dryness scale (see Tasting 2). The Californian wine will also be very dry, but the more fruity wines can seem sweeter.

CHAMPAGNE METHOD

The first stages in the production of Champagne are very much the same as in the production of any other wine and indeed, until the mid-eighteenth century, Champagne was a still wine.

Then Dom Pérignon, who is credited with inventing Champagne as it is now, had the idea of creating a second fermentation in the bottle which would give the wine life and fizz. Extra-strength English glass bottles and wired corks from Spain were brought in to withstand the increased pressure.

Today, the still wines are blended and bottled and then a solution of sugar, wine and yeast or *liqueur de tirage* is added. The wine is then corked and stored in a cool cellar. A secondary fermentation takes place in the bottle, leaving carbon dioxide dissolved in the wine. At this point the wine is left to rest and mature for a while.

During this time the dead yeasts fall out of the wine and have to be removed. This is done by a process called *rémuage*. The bottles are turned, tapped and replaced in their racks at a slightly different angle every day. The work is carried out in such a way that, after about three months, the bottles end up neck down. The neck of each bottle is plunged into a bath of freezing brine and the yeasty sludge turns into an ice pellet that is quickly removed. This process is known as *dégorgement*.

The wine is now completely dry and not all that pleasant to drink, though there are those who like it. The last step is to sweeten the wine a little with the *dosage*, a mixture of sugar and wine. The amount of *dosage* that is added determines exactly how sweet the wine will be.

Champagne is labeled, in ascending order of sweetness Brut, Extra Dry, Sec (dry), Demi-Sec (medium) and Doux (sweet). In practice Brut wines can vary from very dry to medium dry.

You may be surprised by how much the two wines have in common. If there are differences it could well be due to the fact that the French Champagne has more older wines in its blend than the California wine. The Champagne will be a blend of eight or ten wines, but because this type of wine is fairly new to California, producers don't have the same stock from which to create their wines.

If you think that the wines are very similar, why not taste them again at the end of this session? But instead of looking at the labels, pour wines for each other in such a way that you do not know which is which. Can you tell them apart now?

THE CHOICE OF SPARKLING WINES

Some sparkling wines made by the Champagne houses in other parts of the world may come close to emulating Champagne, but the majority of sparkling wines are quite different. Although they share the traditional method of production, they are made from different grape varieties, grown on different soils and in different climates. As a result they have their own style and are good wines in their own right.

Pour the Cava (wine C) and make a note on the color, aromas and flavors you find.

Cava comes from Penedès, where there is a tradition of making sparkling wine that is at least as old as that in Champagne. There are some who say that Dom Pérignon got his ideas from the Spaniards of Penedès!

Cava is usually fairly pale in color. What kind of descriptive words have you used for the nose? You can

---

FRENCH SPARKLING WINES

Here are some other French AC sparkling wines that you might like to taste another time:

Blanquette de Limoux: This wine comes from the Limoux area near Carcassonne in southwest France. It is made from the local Mauzac grape with some Chenin Blanc and Chardonnay. The wine is made using the traditional Champagne method.

Clairette de Die Tradition: This wine comes from the southern Rhône region of France. It is made from the local Clairette grape and the Muscat grape. The sparkle in this grapey wine comes not from secondary fermentation but from a prolonged continuation of the first fermentation. The wine is filtered and bottled when there is still some unfermented sugar left in it, which subsequently provides the bubbles without any extra yeast or sugar having to be added. It has a very fruity aroma and flavor.

Clairette de Die Brut: This wine is made from the Clairette grape and is not as interesting as the Tradition style. By 1998 these wines will be renamed Crémant de Die and Crémant de Die Tradition.

Saumur Mousseux or Saumur d'Origine: Saumur is the center of the sparkling wine industry of the Loire. The wines are made in the traditional way from a range of grape varieties including Chenin Blanc, Chardonnay, Sauvignon Blanc, Gamay, Cabernet Franc and Cabernet Sauvignon.

Vouvray Mousseux: This wine is made by the traditional Champagne method in Vouvray on the north bank of the Loire in central France. The grape variety is Chenin Blanc.

Grandes Marques quite literally means "great brands" and in Champagne the term is used to describe houses that belong to the Syndicat de Grandes Marques de Champagnes. At one time their products were considered to be the very best Champagnes. Today their quality is more variable and there are some very good producers who are not members. The Grandes Marques are Ayala, Billecart-Salmon, Bollinger, Canard Duchêne, Deutz & Geldermann, Heidsieck Monopole, Charles Heidsieck, Henriot, Krug, Lanson, Laurent-Perrier, Massé Père et Fils, Mercier, Moët & Chandon, Montebello, Mumm, Perrier-Jouët, Joseph Perrier, Piper-Heidsieck, Pol Roger, Pommery & Greno, Prieur, Louis Roederer, Ruinart, Salon, Taittinger, and Veuve Clicquot.

RED SPARKLING WINES

Red sparkling wines are quite rare but they do exist. Lambrusco from Emilia-Romagna in Italy is perhaps the best-known example. Ordinary Lambrusco, without DOC status, is semi-fizzy and usually very sweet, lacking good balancing acidity. Rather better if you can find it is Lambrusco DOC which is much more refreshing and fruity.

If you are interested in experimenting with red sparklers you could try Saumur Mousseux Rouge from France, Australian Sparkling Shiraz made by Seppelt and Charles Melton wineries, or Australian Sparkling Cabernet from Yalumba winery.

expect a good Cava to have a fresh lemony aroma and a full nutty flavor. It will also have some light earthy tones which are not unpleasant, although in inferior brands this earthy smell is less attractive, becoming almost mushroomy.

Cava is not as acid as Champagne and not quite as dry, but most are labeled Brut and are classed at the 1 to 2 level on the European sweetness scale. The wine was traditionally made from three Spanish grape varieties—Parallada, Xarello and Viura—none of which have particular varietal flavors. Today, producers are starting to add some Chardonnay to the mix; one or two wines are made purely from this grape variety and on these you may pick up some honey or buttery flavors.

Pour the French *crémant* (wine D) and make a note on the color, aromas and flavors you find.

The regions of Saumur, Alsace and Burgundy have been producing sparkling wine for many years and, though their provenance is not as old as that of Champagne, they have developed their own tastes and styles. Your French sparkler may not have much more color than the Cava.

You may find that the aromas and flavors of the grape varieties in the French *crémant* wines are more obvious than in the Cava. Crémant de Loire is made predominantly from the Chenin Blanc grape, which is a particularly acidic variety. At its best it produces very fresh wines with attractive honeyed overtones and a characteristic aroma of wet wool. Chardonnay sometimes turns up in these wines too—whether you identify it in your sample will depend upon which producer's wine you have chosen.

Expect the Crémant d'Alsace to have more flowery
fruit. Producers may use any of the grapes of Alsace
with the exception of Gewürztraminer, which has too
definite a flavor to go into a blend. In practice this
means that Pinot Blanc is the leading grape variety
used, although there may be some Riesling in the
mix. The more of this latter variety there is in the
blend the more flowery the flavor of the wine.

Chardonnay is the predominant grape variety used
for Crémant de Bourgogne. It often has a slightly
toasty woody aroma and flavor. Sometimes it is
blended with Pinot Noir and occasionally the resulting
wine can almost be mistaken for Champagne. What
did you think about the *crémant* you chose?

**Pour the new world sparkler (wine E) and
make a note on the color, aromas and flavors
you find.**

Chardonnay is also likely to be the predominant grape
variety in the more expensive new world sparklers.

ITALIAN SPARKLING WINES

Moscato Spumante is made from the same grape
variety and in the same way as Asti Spumante and
comes from the same region. However, it is made
outside the designated area or DOC.
Prosecco is a wine made from a grape variety of the
same name in northeast Italy. The most popular style
is made in the traditional Champagne manner. It may
be semi-dry or medium sweet, and is light and fruity.

This certainly does not mean that
they all taste the same, but it does
mean that they tend to be softer and
more fruity than many of their
European counterparts. The new
world wine, in line with many of
the still wines, could well have a
more definite yellow cast to it.

Each winery has its own
style, but good Australian
sparkling wine is fresh with
lemony fruit and the tropical
fruit flavors so characteristic of
this part of the world. Those
producers who use Chardonnay
are also experimenting with the
use of Pinot Noir and blending
older vintages into the wine. The
results are rapidly improving
wines with more complex
flavors.

Californian sparkling wines are often heavier than
their counterparts in Australia, tending towards dry
yeasty aromas with less fruit. However, techniques are
changing here too and tomorrow's sparkling wines
could be quite different.

**Which wine do you like the best? Discuss
your findings with the other tasters. Add your
conclusions to your notes for future reference.**

So far in this tasting you have been sampling dry
Champagne and dry sparkling wines, but by no means
are all good sparkling wines dry.

Pour the Asti Spumante (wine F).

This is perhaps the most popular sparkling wine in the world after Champagne. It is made from the Moscato or Italian Muscat grape. The producers use a *cuve close* method of production rather than the traditional one, but because of its unique features the wine is always very fresh and fruity.

Juice is extracted from the grapes after the harvest, filtered and chilled to 0°C. It remains at this temperature until the wine is wanted in the marketplace. The required amount of juice is then warmed and partly fermented in an open tank. The tanks are then closed to allow the wine to gain its bubbles. Finally it is bottled under pressure.

This system ensures that the wine is as fresh as it possibly can be when bottled and it should be drunk immediately; Asti Spumante is not intended to mature. The older it is the less enjoyable it will be.

CALIFORNIA SPARKLERS

Schramsberg is probably the best-known producer of sparkling wine in California and is certainly the oldest. Proprietors Jack and Jamie Davies began producing wine using the traditional method in the late sixties and early seventies. Today, sparking wine is made state-wide. The Korbel winery produces crisp sparkling wines in the Russian River Valley region of Sonoma County. Sparking wines from Washington State—particularly those made by the Château Ste. Michelle winery—are receiving increasing attention.

Begin by looking at the color and appearance of the wine.

Asti Spumante is a pretty pale yellow. The bubbles may be a little larger than those of the other wines you have sampled, but there should still be a good rush of them.

Now make a note on the aromas you find. It will certainly be very fruity, but what kind of fruit and how intense is this aroma?

Good Asti Spumante retains the full aroma and flavor of the Moscato grape, which is unmistakably grapey but it has a fruit salad of aromas. You may find mangoes, strawberries, grapefruit and many others, but the wine should also be apple fresh. You may smell hints of honey and spices, too, but there will be no wood or vanilla oak.

Finally make notes on the palate of the wine. How sweet is it and is it balanced by good acidity?

This wine retains much of the natural sugar of the grapes so expect a sweet taste. Asti Spumante is usually classed as medium sweet to sweet (7 to 8 on the European sweetness scale). In a good wine this sweetness is balanced by good acidity. The wine should have a light velvety texture, but should not be in the least bit cloying or unpleasant. The finish should be as pleasant as the mouthful itself.

Expect an easy-drinking wine with no bitterness. The alcohol level is a low seven to eight percent by volume. Despite its distinctively grapey flavor, Asti Spumante makes a very good pudding wine and will partner a wide range of desserts.

WINE AND FOOD

Wine and food are natural partners, but can you serve any wine with any food? The uninitiated will say "why not?" and the wine snob will give a resounding "No you cannot." The real answer lies between these two extremes.

If you like a certain wine there is no reason why you should not serve it at any meal. But if you make the effort to think about how the flavors of the wine and food work together you might find that some are more successful than others.

This is because the properties of the wine react with the properties of the food. Sometimes this intermingling produces something even better than the individual flavors and you have a great match. Sometimes the opposite happens.

There used to be hard and fast rules about which wines should be served with which foods and at what stage of the meal. The modern approach is to consider the properties of the wine and match these to the type of food to be served.

The body of the wine, its fruit, acidity, tannin, wood and sweetness level will all affect the way it will interact with the food. A heavy wine will swamp the delicate flavor of trout and a sweet wine will make a drier dish seem harsh and austere. A spicy dish will overpower the taste of a fine Burgundy, whereas a simple grilled steak will show the wine off to perfection.

The foods have been chosen to illustrate the general effect of different types of food on the taste and appreciation of wine. They include an acid food (slices of tomato), a fatty food (buttered bread), a well-flavored and fatty food (slices of salami), a spicy meat dish (chili con carne). If you have the time, make two chilies, one hotter than the other. Do the tasting first with the mild dish, then the stronger one. Compare the effect each has on the wine.

THE EFFECT OF FOOD ON THE TASTE OF WINE

Pour all five wines and taste them in the order in which they are listed. Make full notes on the color, nose and palate of each wine, concentrating particularly on their acid, fruit and tannin levels.

The white wines (wines A and B) have been specially chosen to exhibit high acidity with light spicy fruit on the one hand, and intensely lush ripe and oily fruit on the other. The first red (wine C) should be simple, fresh and

THE WINES

A. A DRY WHITE WINE WITH A HIGH ACIDITY

B. A DRY, BUT VERY FRUITY WHITE WINE

C. A SIMPLE FRUITY RED WINE WITH LITTLE OR NO TANNIN

D. A VERY TANNIC RED WINE

Here are some suggestions:

A. MUSCADET *, GROS PLANT, SAUVIGNON DE TOURAINE *, ITALIAN PINOT GRIGIO

B. CHARDONNAY *, SEMILLON OR CHARDONNAY/SEMILLON *from California, New Zealand, Australia or South Africa*

C. VALPOLICELLA *, BEAUJOLAIS *, YOUNG CALIFORNIA PINOT NOIR, FRENCH VIN DE PAYS *, GAMAY * OR LIGHT BLENDED CALIFORNIA RED *

D. CROZES-HERMITAGE *, BAROLO * OR DÃO *

You will also need:

E. THE FRUITIEST AUSTRALIAN SHIRAZ OR CALIFORNIA ZINFANDEL YOU CAN FIND

★You may have some of these wines left over from previous tastings

fruity, the second (wine D) big and tannic, and the third (wine E) big and fruity.

Check first of all that the wines do exhibit the characteristics suggested above. If they do not taste quite as you expected them to taste, make a special note to that effect. At the end of the session you can check the label and any back label to see why this bottle is different to other wines from the same region.

Now eat a little of the salami with the bread and butter then taste wine A again. **How does the food affect the taste of the wine? Does it seem as acidic as it did on first tasting? What has happened to the flavor of the wine?**

You may find that the acidity is unchanged, as the bread itself is fairly neutral and the meat does not have too much acidity of its own. Indeed, the acidity of the wine should be a good contrast to the rich fattiness of the salami. If you chose the Sauvignon de Touraine, how did its very definite flavor work with the meat?

Taste wine A with the tomato and bread and butter. Is the acidity affected now?

Savory dishes that contain even small amounts of acidic ingredients, such as tomatoes, apples, citrus fruits, or their juice, need wines with good acidity to match them, because they can make a wine with low acidity seem dull and flat. This is true not just for dishes such as pork and orange casserole or cranberry pot roast, but also for roasted and grilled or broiled meats served with fruity stuffings or sauces.

However, wine A should easily have sufficient acidity to deal with the tomatoes in these sand-wiches and the match could well be a good one. What do you think?

Eat some more of the tomato sandwich and taste wine B. Is there enough acidity in this wine to withstand the tomatoes, and how is its fruity flavor affected?

Check your earlier notes on the acidity level of this wine then reassess it in the light of the effect the tomatoes are having. If the wine has good acidity it should stand up to the sandwiches. Fruity foods need fruity flavors in wine to match them, so you may find that wine B performs better on this level than wine A.

You might also like to try tasting the tomato slices on their own with the wines to see whether the bread and butter has had a "cushioning" effect.

Now try wines C and D with a bite of the salami and the tomato sandwiches. Consider the effect of the food on the tannin as well as the acidity and fruitiness of the wines. Which sandwich goes best with which wine?

The tomato sandwich could be a good match for wine C. There is little or no tannin in the wine, but the final partnership will depend upon whether or not the fruity flavors match each other. If they do not the match will still fail.

Both sandwiches are likely to have a softening effect on the strong tannins in wine D. Tannin has a similar cutting effect on fatty food as acidity, so you may find that wine D works rather better with the salami sandwich than wine C.

Tannin in wine does not always work well with food. Some people avoid red wine with fish dishes because the combination of tannins and fish can result in an unpleasant metallic taste in the mouth. However, others do not experience this at all and enjoy the combination, particularly with meatier fish such as tuna, swordfish, sardines, or salmon.

Other mild foods such as veal and chicken in white sauce, farm-raised duck and turkey can be over-whelmed by very tannic wines. But not all red wines are aggressively tannic and there is no reason why lighter red wines should not be served with these meats.

"DIFFICULT" FOODS

There are some foods that are difficult to match because they have very specific flavors that often clash with those of the wine. Vinegar is one of these. Raw vinegar and wine just do not mix, so use plenty of oil in your vinaigrette dressings and keep the vinegar to a minimum if you are serving wine at a meal. Better still, replace the vinegar with a little lemon juice. Dishes cooked with vinegar are less of a problem as the vinegar evaporates, but you will need good acidity in the accompanying wine.

Artichokes are notoriously difficult to match, particularly if they are served with butter or oil. Try Champagne, which goes with most things, or use the artichokes in a salad with other ingredients and drink a lush Chardonnay. In Italy chefs slice the raw vegetable very thinly and serve them with slivers of Parmesan cheese, lemon juice and olive oil. The suggested wine is often an acidic but fruity northern Italian red such as Barbera d'Asti.

Asparagus with butter or oil can also present problems. Expert tasters do sometimes compare the aroma of certain wines to asparagus, so have a look through your notes to see if you have used this description. If you have, you may find that this is the wine to serve. Alternatively try a chilled fino sherry or a crisp Italian white wine such as Galestro from Tuscany or Verdicchio from the Marches.

Smoked salmon can give a metallic, extra-fishy flavor to wine. Try an oaky Chardonnay or a sparkling wine of some kind. Dry amontillado sherry can be very good too.

MATCHING FOOD AND WINE

In the days when people sat down to long formal dinners there were quite elaborate rules about the kind of wine to serve at each course. As a result, the general rule of thumb that white wine should be served with fish and red wine with meat and cheese came into being. However, in traditional wine-producing regions the locals quite happily drink white wine with meat or cook their fish in red wine—it all depends on the type of wine made in the area.

So how do you find a combination of wine and food that works? Firstly, you must decide whether it is the wine or the food that is to be showcased. If you want to show off your best wine or a new or unusual "find," your approach will be very different than if you want to show off your cooking skills.

Simply cooked dishes made with first-class ingredients are the best foil for great wines. Grilled fish or chicken, roast lamb or beef, or plain hamburgers are good examples. As soon as you add sauces and other trimmings you start to complicate the taste signals and this can detract from the wine. On the other hand, if your unusual find is very robust it may need more complexity in the meal to cope with its concentrated flavors and high tannin levels.

Pour wines C, D and E and serve the chili con carne.

These wines include a light fruity red wine (wine C), a very tannic wine (wine D) and a much fuller but still fruity wine (wine E). The dish is a deliberately hot and spicy one.

THE LOWER HUNTER VALLEY OF AUSTRALIA

Taste wines C and E with the chili and make a note on the effect that the food has on the fruitiness and acidity of the wines.

Does the fruit stand up to the onslaught of the chili? If you can still taste the light red wine (wine C) you are doing quite well, but it is sure to be pleasant and refreshing even if you are losing some of the fruit. Lively fresh wine can help to tone down the chili making it a good choice to partner hot spicy food.

An even better choice might be wine E, the Zinfandel or Shiraz. The vibrant fruit extract in these wines will often stand up to the strong and spicy flavors of even a hot dish like chili con carne. How does your example measure up to this?

The higher the acidity level of the wine the more likely it is to make a refreshing accompaniment to spicy food. How do these wines score here?

🍷 **Taste wine D with the chili.**

Hot spicy food will certainly soften harsh or tannic wines such as this one, and make what fruit there is more accessible. Indeed, this is a good way of drinking up wines with which you were disappointed.

How does your tannic wine fare with this dish? If it is a good example of its kind its complexity of flavor will be lost amid the heat of the dish.

APPROACHES TO MATCHING FOOD AND WINE

You can choose a wine to complement the flavors in the food, or choose a contrasting wine that will stand up to those flavors. Ask yourself the following questions about the main course.
• Is the main dish plainly cooked, or does it have a variety of strong flavors competing for attention? If so, it will need an equally aggressive wine to match it.
• Does the food contain any very acid ingredients, such as vinegar, fruits and tomatoes, that should be

EAST MEETS WEST ON THE PACIFIC COAST

Today some of the most innovative food has a Pacific rim influence. The fresh clean flavors of Japan, and the sharp flavors of Vietnam and Thailand can all be matched with a little experimentation. Try a Chenin Blanc or Fumé Blanc with Japanese dishes, and California Riesling or Alsatian Gewürztraminer with the sweeter Chinese or Thai flavors.

matched by the acidity in the wine?
• Are there any very fruity or other definite flavors in the food that need to be matched by the wine?
• Is the dish a fatty or oily one? Does it need to be cut by a wine with a high level of acidity?
• Are there any sweet ingredients in the dish that will rule out the choice of a very dry wine?
• Has the food been cooked with wine? If it has, you should try to serve the same or at least a similar style of wine with it.

In practice this means thinking about the ingredients, cooking method, and accompaniments of the main dish you are planning to serve. Thus, if you are planning to serve barbecued chicken with a fruity, sweet-sour baste you should consider serving a full-bodied fruity wine with good acidity. Avoid anything too crisp and dry as it will taste very harsh.

With these criteria in mind you might go for a good California or Australian Chardonnay with plenty of tropical pineapple flavors, or a rich red Rioja. On the other hand, you might prefer the contrast of an acidic but intensely flavored Pouilly-Fumé or Sancerre, or a fruity Chianti Classico.

If you decide to serve more than one wine with a meal, the order in which you serve them could make a big difference to your guests' enjoyment. Serve young wines before more mature wines—if you drink them the other way round the mature wine can make the younger one seem spiky and gauche. Serve drier and lighter wines before those that are aromatic and sweeter, as sweet wines make drier ones taste extremely astringent.

MIX AND MATCH

Matching food and wine is fun and it should not be taken overly seriously. The more you concentrate on matching wines to specific foods the more it will become evident that there is no such thing as one perfect wine for a dish. There are often several wines that will partner a dish very well, but thinking in greater depth about food and wine combinations will encourage you to be more adventurous, and this in turn will introduce you to new taste experiences.

Deciding on the best food and wine combination can be difficult as people's tastebuds do not always react in the same way. Your favorite may be another taster's last choice.

As we saw in Tasting 11, one of the most important considerations in matching wine and food is the intensity or delicacy of the flavors. Well-flavored or rich foods need full-bodied wines with good fruit and acidity. You will also need to consider how the flavors of the food will affect the wood flavors and the tannins of the wine.

This consideration of the interaction of flavors applies when matching wine and cheese. Tannin, particularly, can be a problem with some cheeses. However, there is no reason why an appropriate white wine should not be served with cheese. Indeed sweet white wine partners blue cheese extremely well.

The foods have been chosen to illustrate an approach to matching wine to a range of main courses, cheeses and the ever-problematic chocolate dessert. They are:

1 Pasta with your favorite tomato and meat sauce, grilled steak, or fried chicken.
2 Soft creamy cheese such as Camembert or Brie; a hard Cheddar-style cheese; blue cheese such as Stilton, Roquefort or Gorgonzola.
3 Chocolate dessert such as mousse or torte.

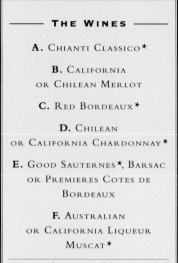

THE WINES

A. CHIANTI CLASSICO★

B. CALIFORNIA OR CHILEAN MERLOT

C. RED BORDEAUX★

D. CHILEAN OR CALIFORNIA CHARDONNAY★

E. GOOD SAUTERNES★, BARSAC OR PREMIERES COTES DE BORDEAUX

F. AUSTRALIAN OR CALIFORNIA LIQUEUR MUSCAT★

★You may have some of these wines left over from previour tastings

MATCHING WINE TO FOOD

Pour wines A, B and C. If you would like to include a white wine, pour wine D and taste this first. Make full notes on the color, nose and palate of each wine.

Once you have made a full assessment of the wines, serve the dish you have chosen from Food 1.

Take a bite of the food then try wine D. Write notes on how the food has affected the taste of the wine. Try the rest of the wines with the food and write notes in just the same way.

What has happened to the fruit, woods and tannins in the wines? For example, if you chose the pasta how

are the full fruity flavors of the new world white (wine D) standing up to the tomatoes in the sauce? Does the acidity level of the Chianti Classico (wine A) complement that of the food? What do you think about drinking a red Bordeaux (wine C) or a new world Merlot with this type of food?

Wine producers have traditionally made wines to accompany their local or national cuisine so you may find that the Chianti is the best choice to accompany the pasta. If you like cooking in the Mediterranean style you may like to carry this through into your wine choices. Thus you might choose to serve a Provençal dish with a Country wine from the South of France, or a Spanish dish with Rioja.

Consider the same factors of fruitiness, wood and tannin if you have chosen to serve the steak. In theory, the Bordeaux red (wine C) should come into its own here as this is one of the classic European partnerships. Do you agree with the recommendation, or do you prefer the lush fruit of the two new world wines (wines B and D)? How did the Chianti (wine A) fare?

The wine with the highest acidity levels may well be the best partner for the fried chicken because it will be able to deal with the rich coating and the fat from the frying process.

Which wine do you think best partners the food? Discuss your findings with the other tasters if you are tasting in a group. If there is a consensus record it in your notebook.

MATCHING WINE AND CHEESE

Wine and cheese is a great combination, but you cannot pick a wine and a cheese at random and automatically expect them work well together. There are traditional guidelines for mixing and matching wine and cheese and these can be useful, but there are also plenty of unorthodox yet delicious combinations that you will only find by experimenting. The traditional approach to matching wine with cheese, particularly in Europe, was to choose a relatively austere classic red wine like the Bordeaux red (wine C) regardless of the cheese to be served. The idea of serving white wine with cheese is relatively new.

Pour wines B, C, D and E, making full notes on the color, nose and palate of each one. **Now taste the Chardonnay (wine D) with the soft cheese.**

Cheeses like Camembert and Brie have a definite flavor of their own, but are relatively mild compared to hard cheese or blue cheese. They have a creamy texture and a fruity, sometimes slightly moldy flavor. They should not be so ripe that they smell of ammonia.

How did you find the Chardonnay and soft cheese partnership? Did the buttery oiliness of the Chardonnay complement the rich taste and soft texture of the soft rind cheeses, or did you find the combination too unctious? Do you think that a less fulsome Chardon-

FONTODI VINEYARD IN CHIANTI

nay from one of the French Vin de Pays regions or northern Italy might partner the cheese better?

Now that you have tasted this combination you may well decide there is no reason that white wine cannot be served alongside of cheese.

Try the same cheese with wines C and B. **Which partnership do you prefer and how did they compare with the Chardonnay and soft cheese combination?**

Do you think the Bordeaux (wine C) goes well with this cheese, or do you prefer the fuller fruitiness of the new world Merlot? Does one flavor dominate the other or is there a marriage of flavors?

Think about how the acidity levels of the two wines cope with the creamy texture of the cheese. Soft cheese usually needs good acidity in its accompanying wines. How are the tannin levels affecting the partnership? You may find that the cheese makes a wine with high tannin levels seem very dry.

Discuss your findings with the other tasters and see if you can come to a consensus on the best type of wine to serve with this kind of cheese.

Serve the Cheddar-style cheese next and taste it with wine D. Does the Chardonnay go with this cheese as well as it did with the soft rind cheese?

TASTING SUGGESTION

If you like the idea of serving white wine with cheese here are some combinations you might like to try:

Soft creamy cheese with German Riesling Kabinett

Goat's cheese with Sancerre, Sauvignon de Touraine or California Fumé Blanc

Semi-hard cheese with Australian Rhine Riesling

Soft creamy cheese with Champagne or California sparkling wine

Mature Cheddar with Sauvignon Blanc from New Zealand

Smoked cheese with a very oaky Chardonnay.

Hard Cheddar-style cheeses have an interesting nutty flavor that strengthens as the cheese matures. A powerfully flavored cheese will easily swamp a light wine such as Muscadet or Pinot Grigio. How does your wine stand up to this challenge? The flavors of the cheese and of the wine may remain separate, or you may find that they combine to form something less pleasant than the individual flavors.

Now serve the same cheese with wines C and B. Which do you prefer?

Cheddar-style cheeses are very tolerant of tannin in wine. In fact, they are relatively easy to match and both these wines should be acceptable. You may find that the cheese actually enhances the fruit in the Bordeaux (wine C). Or you may prefer the soft, fruity flavors of the new world red with the cheese.

However, the partnership will be affected by the maturity of the cheese that you have chosen and, indeed, by the age of the wine. Neither is a static product; they both mature over time with consequent changes in flavor and texture. Thus the results will be different with a young cheese to those you will get if you have a more mature example. Often younger wines partner young cheeses better than more mature wines.

Serve the blue cheese with wines C and B. Which partnership do you prefer?

The distinctive flavor of blue cheese comes from the blue or green molds that vein the paste. Though blue

In Europe, where a separate cheese course is served at formal dinners, there is some debate over whether the cheese should be served before or after the dessert.

The English tradition of serving cheese after the dessert grew out of an Elizabethan belief that "cheese closed the stomach" and should thus be served at the end of the meal. Port was plentiful and, once the combination was discovered, became the natural accompaniment to cheese.

The French like to serve red wine with their cheese and it makes sense for them to continue serving whatever red wine accompanied the main course. Anything sweet served between the main course and the cheese would make a subsequent red wine taste dusty and astringent.

Which approach is the most appropriate depends largely upon the type of wine you wish to serve.

cheese may seem creamier than a Cheddar-style cheese, their fat content of 48 percent is the same. Like other cheeses its flavors increase in complexity as they mature.

In England Stilton was known as the king of cheese and the traditional wine to serve with it was red Bordeaux. In France the king of cheese was considered to be Roquefort, but the choice of wine was still red Bordeaux. If you have chosen one of these cheeses what do you think about the traditional combination?

How does the blue cheese and red Bordeaux partnership compare with the blue cheese and new world

wine partnership? How does the full fruity flavor of the wine cope with the flavor of the cheese? You may find that you do not like either of them. It all depends upon the cheese you have chosen.

Now taste the same cheese with wine E. Do you think that this combination works?

The idea of serving a sweet wine with blue cheese may seem rather strange at first, but in France, where Roquefort reigns supreme, this partnership is commonplace and in England sweet wine, in the form of port, was the traditional partner for Stilton.

Even if you have not chosen Roquefort or Stilton you should still find the combination of blue cheese and Sauternes interesting. The more acidic the cheese and the sharper its flavor the more it will balance the full body and sweetness of the Sauternes. Mature Stilton may not be quite sour enough to partner this wine.

Discuss your findings with the other tasters and make a note of the results.

Make a note every time you experiment with a wine and cheese combination as the knowledge you gain will be useful for planning menus in the future. If you do find a perfect match, resist the temptation to add another couple of cheeses to your selection. The problem with a mixed cheese board is that the wine must be chosen to match the mildest cheese. The flavor of the strongest cheese may swamp the wine, and if the wine is too strong the same fate will befall the milder cheeses, which might just as well not be there at all. It is perfectly acceptable to serve a single carefully chosen cheese with a well-matched wine.

MATCHING WINE AND CHOCOLATE

Pour wines D, E and F. Taste wine F, making full notes on the color, nose and palate of the wine.

This fortified wine should have a strong and complex aroma of dried apricots, grapes and raisins, and maybe even caramel. It will have a high alcohol content, and this seems to intensify the aromas and flavors. Good examples will have a reasonable level of acidity.

Now clear your palate with some sparkling water and perhaps a plain cracker. Take a spoonful of your chosen chocolate dessert, then try wine D.

WINES TO TRY WITH CHOCOLATE DESSERTS

All kinds of wines have been suggested to go with chocolate desserts. However, those made from the Muscat grape are often the best because this grape variety manages to keep its fresh flavor whatever it is served with. Here are some Muscat-based wines to try:
• Asti Spumante
• Muscat de Beaumes de Venise
• Muscat de Rivesaltes
• Moscatel de Valencia
Another wine worth trying is Banyuls from the South of France, which is made from the red Grenache grape. An unusual combination is that of California Cabernet Sauvignon with chocolate—a pairing that has gained favor with some American critics.

Chocolate desserts are usually very sweet and this rules out serving it with any but the sweetest wines. The Chardonnay may have plenty of lush ripe fruit, but it is a dry wine and your dessert will kill its wonderful flavor. It may even taste quite astringent.

Take another spoonful of the chocolate dessert and this time follow it with wine E. Is this a better match?

This combination should taste better than the last one. How pleasant it is will depend upon the dessert you are serving. Some are sweet, but the chocolate flavor may not be overpowering and the Sauternes may well stand up to them.

However, if you have chosen a really rich chocolate cheesecake or Mississippi Mud Pie, the chocolate flavors will be much stronger and you may find that the Sauternes is totally swamped. All the sweet fruit flavors will disappear and you may be left just with the acidity.

Finally taste the chocolate dessert with wine F. Do you like this partnership? Is it better or worse than that with wine E?

The unusual combination of fresh grapes and dried fruits in the Liqueur Muscat could well be the answer to the difficulties of matching chocolate. With luck both tastes will survive and blend into a new and interesting flavor combination.

HOW GRAPES ARE GROWN AND VINIFIED

Grapes can be grown in only two bands around the world: between the latitudes of 50°N and 30°N in the northern hemisphere and in a similar band in the southern hemisphere. Beyond these limits the climate is too hot to allow the vines a resting period in the winter, or too cold for the grapes to ripen properly.

Within these areas the best vineyards are sited on well-drained but poor soils. Each variety of grape has its own preferred soil base, but slate, gravel, limestone and chalk all yield soils that are ideally suited to viniculture. The poorer the soil and the better drained it is the further the roots have to penetrate to find moisture and nourishment. The result is a stable environment deep below the surface that enables the vines to withstand the rigours above ground.

Dry soils are warmer soils and some, like chalk and limestone, also reflect the heat of the sun back up to the plant. This is important in cool climates where vineyards will be sited on slopes that catch the sun at the warmest time of the day. In hotter climates, vineyards frequently face away from the sun. The "aspect" or angle at which the sun hits a vineyard is crucial to the successful cultivation of top quality grapes. The best vineyards are often situated on the south or southwest facing slopes of a hillside.

MANUAL HARVESTING

The density in which the vines are planted also depends upon the climate. If there is likely to be very little rain the vines will be planted further apart than if the region is a wet one.

Clay and other rich, heavy soils can be used to grow grapes quite successfully in the hotter regions of the world.

THE VINEYARD YEAR

Before the grapes reach the winery the grower will have invested a year of hard work, trying to keep the vines in good condition and bring the right quantity of grapes to their optimum level of ripeness for harvesting. In the northern hemisphere the year begins after the vintage in late September, October or early November, and in the southern hemisphere in February or March.

During the winter months, when the temperature drops to about 52°F/11°C, the grapes go into a dormant phase. Unless the temperature falls below -28°F/-18°C, the grapes will survive.

This is the time to begin pruning the vines. Pruning is carried out to control quality and quantity. Long branches are cut off first, then in December or January each vine is cut back more severely. The level of pruning will determine the yield the following year. An experienced pruner will assess each vine and its potential separately. Late winter is also the time to take cuttings that will be grafted onto new rootstock to plant out new vineyards or replace old ones.

The winter months are the time for general tidying, plowing and manuring of the vineyards. In cooler areas soil is banked up round the base of each vine to protect the roots. Soil that has been washed downhill to lower vineyards during the year is carted back to those higher up.

In spring last minute pruning is completed and the soil is worked again to uncover the roots and allow the air to reach them. As new shoots grow they are trained up wires or trellises in complicated patterns according to local customs. This step is followed by the first spraying with pesticides. Vines are prone to various diseases so spraying continues through the summer to the harvest.

MACHINE HARVESTING

An attack by Phylloxera vastatrix is a disaster for a vineyard. Phylloxera is a parasitic louse that attacks the roots of the vine. It is controlled by grafting European vines onto American rootstocks, which are resistant to it. However, this resistance is waning and Phylloxera is now attacking vines grafted in this way.

Frost in April or May, when the first leaf shoots and flower buds appear, can kill the vines. In some areas, such as Chablis in France, the Rhine Valley in Germany, and the Napa Valley in California, growers use stoves, flame guns and torches to warm up the air. They also use giant propellers to stop frozen air sliding into nooks and hollows. In some places the vines are continually sprayed with water which freezes to ice and so keeps the temperature round the shoots at zero.

In summer, flowering and pollination are crucial. If it rains during the ten- to fourteen-day period when the vines are in flower they may not be pollinated and the fruit will not set, thus drastically reducing the yield. Once flowering is over the vines may be thinned to remove excessive growth and to allow more sunshine to reach the grapes. The growing bunches of grapes, too, may be thinned. Growers continue to spray the vines and hope for dry weather. Warm, wet weather can herald the onset of rot, and a hailstorm can decimate a vineyard in less than an hour.

As the grapes reach maturity in the autumn and the sugar levels are measured, efforts are made to ward off any last minute diseases or insect invasions. Birds must be kept away as they can eat the crop before it is picked.

When harvest time is reached, the grapes can be picked laboriously by hand or more quickly by mechanical means. Mechanical harvesters straddle the rows or vines and are both cost-effective and fast, but they are not selective. Thus fine wines and wines affected by noble rot are always picked by hand.

ORGANIC WINES

Organic wine should really be called "wine made from organically grown grapes." Even in those countries that have specific legislation dealing with organic wine, the rules and regulations cover only the cultivation of the grapes—not the production of the wine. They do not, for example, ban the use of Bordeaux mixture, a combination of copper sulfate and lime that is sprayed on vines to protect the grapes from pests. It can turn a vineyard blue.

Organic growers in Europe, America, Australia and New Zealand do not use fertilizers, and they try to keep their use of sprays to a minimum by using biological methods of pest control. However, the line between organic growers and the best of the rest is blurred. There are plenty of ecologically sound vineyards that do not claim to be organic but which would probably fulfill the current organic criteria.

HOW WINE IS MADE

Some growers own their own wineries and so can oversee the progress of their grapes into wine. Others send them to cooperatives or privately owned wineries where grapes from different vineyards are mixed together.

PENFOLD'S WINERY

For much of the year a winery is a relatively quiet place with wine maturing in vats, barrels or bottles, and only routine racking and bottling going on. In the autumn the place becomes a hive of activity.

The first step in the wine-making process is to crush the grapes to release the juices. Traditionally this was done by "treading" the grapes, but today most winemakers use a machine that removes the stems and crushes the grapes at the same time.

The mixture of juice, pips and skins that comes out of the crusher is called the "must." This is emptied into vats or tanks to ferment. Fermentation will take place quite naturally as the yeasts, which were present on the fruit when they were picked, get to work. However, this can be a chancy business and most winemakers add their own cultured yeasts to the must. The mixture may be heated gently to help fermentation begin.

During fermentation the yeasts work on the sugars, which are naturally present in the grapes, and convert them to carbon dioxide and alcohol. Heat is also given off in the reaction, and in hot climates a fermenting vat of wine could soon reach temperatures that would be detrimental to the finished product.

Today, both the temperature of the fermenting wine and the length of fermentation can be controlled in cold-fermentation tanks. A winemaker can produce a light wine by keeping the temperature down, or a fuller, heavier wine with more fruit extract and tannin by fermenting at a higher temperature.

Red grapes are fermented with their skins because it is these that give the wine most of its color. (Peel a red grape and you will see that the flesh is pale green in color.) Tannin is also present, along with some of the fruity flavors. The skins of red grapes are usually kept in the must until fermentation is complete. They tend to form a cap on the surface of the liquid which must be kept on the move to prevent it from drying out.

White wine is usually fermented without the skins, but some producers are experimenting with leaving the skins of white grapes in contact with the juice for a short time to improve the flavors.

WINE MATURING IN OAK

The skins of white grapes are usually separated from the must as soon as they have been crushed. However, in some areas the skins are left in for a while longer to increase the flavors. Most white wines are fermented in large stainless steel tanks and at much lower temperatures than red wines to keep them as fresh and fruity as possible.

At this point the wine can be manipulated to counteract deficiencies in the must. Low sugar levels can be caused by an excess of underripe grapes in the mixture. Chaptalization is used to increase the alcoholic level of wines made from must with low sugar levels. It involves adding sugar during fermentation. This does not sweeten the wine, as the yeasts convert the sugar to alcohol.

Another problem can be low acidity levels, due to the grapes being overripe. Acidity can be added to the fermenting must in the form of tartaric acid, which occurs naturally in grape juice. Alternatively, a form of citric acid can be added at a later stage. Wine that is too acidic may be toned down by adding chalk. The object of these adjustments is to achieve a balanced wine that will taste good and remain stable.

Throughout fermentation care must be taken to prevent the must from "oxidizing" or deteriorating by coming into too much contact with air. This has traditionally been achieved by adding large quantities of sulfur, which can result in a rather unpleasant smell coming out of the bottle as you open it. It is something like the odor that lingers after a match has been struck. Sulfur can also affect the flavor and causes an allergic reaction in some people.

Increasingly a blanket of carbon dioxide is used to protect the wine instead. This too may dissolve into the wine, but its only effect is to give the wine a delicate prickle that will disappear after the wine is opened.

Fermentation stops when all the sugar has been used up, or the alcohol content reaches around 15 percent by volume. This may take three days, three weeks or three months, depending on the temperature within the vats.

After fermentation, red wine is drained off leaving behind a residue that is pressed to extract more wine and the two may then be mixed together. Many red wines are now left to undergo a second non-alcoholic or malolactic fermentation. Bacteria convert the sharp malic acid, naturally present in the grape, to the much milder lactic acid. The wine loses much of its harshness and becomes softer and rounder.

Malolactic fermentation used to take place naturally as the weather warmed up after the harvest. It can now be induced by warming the cellar or injecting the wine with malolactic bacteria. Malolactic fermentation is usually suppressed in white wines so as to preserve their freshness.

Wines for drinking young are stored for a few months in large concrete or stainless steel tanks before bottling. Quality wines may be matured for a little longer in tanks or in wooden casks or barrels. If the winemaker decides to mature his wine in wood he can choose from large wooden vats, small casks made of old oak or small new oak barrels. Each will impart a different flavor to the wine. During this aging process the wine is "racked" or drawn from its sediment and put into clean barrels or containers, leaving the lees behind.

Before the wine is bottled it must be "fined" or clarified with a coagulant such as beaten egg white, gelatine, isinglass, or bentonite which attracts all the impurities and carries them to the bottom as they sink through the wine. It is then racked again and allowed to rest. Some wines are blended at this stage. Blending is carried out to achieve a balanced wine. Depending on the region, the wines may be of the same age or from different vintages. Branded or jug wine is blended from ordinary table wine to achieve a consistent result each year. The label will not specify grape variety or region of origin, although it will usually state the country of origin.

Some wines are also filtered by being passed through a fine mesh to remove solids and bacteria. The process can reduce the flavor of a wine, so some producers leave their wines unfiltered.

Bottling is mostly done on large, automated factory lines, though a few small producers still bottle straight from the cask. Most wine is sold at this stage, but a few fine wines need to mature for a further length of time in the bottle. The finest go on improving for twenty years or more.

GLOSSARY OF TASTING TERMS

These are terms that seek to give a general description of what is in the bottle:

ACIDITY: Acidity gives zest and freshness to a wine and helps to balance sweeter wines that would be cloying without it. Sometimes it tastes like green apples, at others more like lemon or grapefruit juice.

AROMATIC: Fragrant or spicy.

ASTRINGENT: Mouth-puckering. An effect caused by high acidity content.

AUSTERE: Tough and severe with little fruit to balance the wine.

BAKED: "Hot," jammy or earthy smell or taste produced when the grapes have been grown in excessive sunshine with low rainfall.

BALANCED: All of the components of the wine—fruit, acidity, tannin and alcohol—harmonized to create a rounded feel.

BIG: Full of flavor and high in alcohol, tannin, acidity and fruit extract.

BODY: Sensation of the wine in the mouth caused by the fullness of flavor and level of alcohol. Body may be described as light, medium or full.

CHARACTERFUL: Indicates a wine with a distinctive style.

CHEWY: Tannic with lots of flavor.

CLEAN: Free of unpleasant smells.

CLOSED (dumb): Refers to a wine that does not smell or taste as much as you would expect it to. Can be the sign of a very young wine.

CLOYING: Sweet, heavy and lacking in balancing acidity. Leaves an unpleasant sensation in the mouth.

COMPLEX: A wine with many facets.

CRISP: Fresh, but often used as a euphemism for very acidic.

DEPTH: Describes rich flavors that seem to go on for many layers.

ELEGANT: Stylish and refined; the opposite of opulent.

FLABBY: Lacking in acidity and probably with little or no finish.

FLAT: Dull, insipid and lacking acidity, or a sparkling wine that has lost its bubbles.

FLOWERY: Fragrant, perfumed and flower-like.

FRESH: Refers to a wine that retains its attractive youthful acidity.

FRUITY: Refers to the prominent flavor of the grapes, but it does not necessarily mean grapey as in the flavor of fresh table grapes.

GREEN: Suggests unripe fruit, or a raw, young wine.

HARSH OR HARD: Usually refers to a wine that has little fruit and is very tannic.

HERBACEOUS: Reminiscent of grass or herbs.

MELLOW OR MATURE: Wine that has lost its sharp edges and is well rounded.

MEATY: Rich, heavy almost chewy wine.

MOUTH-FILLING: Full-bodied and smooth.

OPULENT: Rich and full-bodied.

PÉTILLANT: Refers to a slight degree of natural sparkle present as tiny bubbles and a faint prickle on the tongue.

RICH: Full-bodied with plenty of fruit extract.

ROBUST: Full-bodied and tough, yet rounded.

SOFT: Usually refers to a wine with quite low acidity.

TANNIC: Refers to a wine that leaves a "furry," harsh impression on the gums and teeth. May soften with age.

TOUGH: Full-bodied with excessive tannin. May be an immature wine that will develop into a great wine in time.

VARIETAL: Refers to the specific grape variety used in a wine. Wines that are labeled with reference to the grape variety are known as "varietal" wines.

VEGETAL: Refers to a general aroma of mature vegetables.

VELVETY: Silky, smooth, often sweet wine.

VINOUS: Pleasant, non-specific winey smell.

PICTURE CREDITS

The publishers would like to thanks the following organizations and individuals for permission to reproduce images:
Cephas Picture Library/Rick England: 116; Steven Morris: 59; R&K Muschenetz: 29; Mick Rock: 20, 21, 30, 34, 37, 45, 48, 53, 55, 57, 63, 69, 71, 77, 85, 89, 94, 95, 96, 105, 109, 113, 114, 115

Frog's Leap Winery/ Meg Smith: 65
Stag's Leap Winery: 40

All the cut-out photographs and chapter openers are by David Armstrong, except for 26, 27, 43, 87 and 93, which are by Karl Adamson.